SERMONETTES FROM THE SEASHORE

SERMONETTES FROM THE SEASHORE

Barry Blackstone

RESOURCE *Publications* • Eugene, Oregon

SERMONETTES FROM THE SEASHORE

Copyright © 2019 Barry Blackstone. All rights reserved. Except for brief quotations in critical publications or reviews, no part of this book may be reproduced in any manner without prior written permission from the publisher. Write: Permissions, Wipf and Stock Publishers, 199 W. 8th Ave., Suite 3, Eugene, OR 97401.

Resource Publications
An Imprint of Wipf and Stock Publishers
199 W. 8th Ave., Suite 3
Eugene, OR 97401

www.wipfandstock.com

PAPERBACK ISBN:978-1-5326-8255-1
HARDCOVER ISBN: 978-1-5326-8256-8
EBOOK ISBN: 978-1-5326-8257-5

Manufactured in the U.S.A.   MARCH 27, 2019

I dedicate these 'sermonettes' to my brother, Michael Blackstone, who shared with me and my family his beach house on long beach island on the Jersey Shore. The renewal we received along that sea edge was just what the Lord ordered after the sudden departure of our son, Scott: that strand of sand inspired this devotional book.

OTHER BOOKS BY BARRY BLACKSTONE

Though None Go With Me

Rendezvous in Paris

Though One Go With Me

Scotland Journey

The Region Beyond

Enlarge My Coast

From Dan to Beersheba and Beyond

The Uttermost Part

Homestead Homilies

Rover: A Boy's Best Friend

North to Alaska and Back

Another Day in Nazareth

CONTENTS

Acknowledgement / ix
Introduction / xi

1. Sea Sovereign / 1
2. Seaside Sermons / 3
3. Southern Sea / 5
4. Kovalam, Kerala / 7
5. Mediterranean Masterpiece / 9
6. Amazing Aqueduct / 11
7. Wave Wisdom / 13
8. Mighty Mystery / 15
9. Southern Sounds / 17
10. Violent Voices / 19
11. Seashore Sunset / 21
12. Solid Sea / 23
13. Herring Hike / 25
14. Turning Tide / 27
15. Bleak Beach / 29
16. Changing Coastlines / 31
17. Eilat Experience / 33
18. Surf Snorkeling / 35
19. Tide Thanksgiving / 37
20. Soaking Storm / 39
21. Divine Design / 41
22. Weathering Winds / 43
23. Cocky Cockleshell / 45
24. Marriage Message / 47
25. Weather's Workshop / 49
26. Beach Borders / 51
27. Beautiful Breakers / 53
28. Beach Benediction / 55
29. Seashore Sorrows / 57
30. Shattered Seawall / 59
31. Barelegged Boy / 61
32. Beautiful Beaches / 63
33. Elegant Eagle / 65
34. Eagle Energy / 67
35. Sea Shore Salmon / 69
36. Shoreline Smorgasbord / 71
37. Scattered Seashells / 73
38. Fashioning Fingers / 75
39. Beach Benefits / 77
40. Tide Therapy / 79
41. Surf Song / 81
42. Salmon Stream / 83
43. Beach Bird / 85
44. "Ebb" Experience / 87
45. Valdez Vista / 89

46. Washing Waves / 91
47. Titanic Thrust / 93
48. Ocean Organ / 95
49. Handyman Handiwork / 97
50. "Life" Lesson / 99
51. Difficult Decision / 101
52. One Ocean / 103
53. Salt Sea / 105
54. Sterile Sea / 107
55. Sea Sunset / 109
56. Galilee Galleon / 111
57. Sea Site / 113
58. Sea Surge / 115
59. Tide's Time / 117
60. Downdraft Disaster / 119
61. Full Flood / 121
62. Sea Sand / 123
63. Sandy Shore / 125
64. Refreshing Reef / 127
65. Wave-Washed / 129
66. Seaside Sermonette / 131
67. Seascape Shaping / 133
68. Sand Sermon / 135
69. Beach Breeze / 137
70. Sand Sculptures / 139
71. Beautiful Breezes / 141
72. Peaceful Places / 143
73. Tranquil Tides / 145
74. Beach Boy / 147
75. Sea Sounds / 149
76. Wave Wreckage / 151
77. Tide Treasure / 153
78. Smooth Sand / 155
79. Titanic Transaction / 157
80. Footstep Footprint / 159
81. California Coast / 161
82. Sea Songs / 163
83. Wave Work / 165
84. Beach Breakers / 167
85. Stilling Storms / 169
86. Changeless Cliff / 171
87. Flying Fowl / 173
88. Fabulous Flowers / 175
89. Smooth Stones / 177
90. Stony Shore / 179
91. Building Breakwaters / 181
92. Southern Storm / 183
93. Tempestuous Tide / 185
94. Hawaii Hop / 187
95. Scott's Seaglass / 189
96. Seashore Sunrise / 191
97. Coastline Conversations / 193
98. Idealic Island / 195

Sermon From The Surf / 197

ACKNOWLEDGEMENTS

I would not have gotten this book project finished if not for the editing and compiling by my friend and sister-in-Christ, Rosemary Campbell. I would like to thank her for the numerous hours and many days she spent reading and correcting the errors in the original script. Thanks again Rosemary for all your work; may you share in the eternal rewards of this book.

INTRODUCTION

I have just returned to the coast of Maine after a three-week sabbatical mourning the death of my first-born child. Scott was just 39 when he departed (II Timothy 4:6) to Glory. The illness that took his physical life was an aggressive lung cancer called Neuroendocrine Carcinoma. It took only six months for this canker to reduce my healthy, 189-pound, six-foot, soldier boy (Scott had spent eight years in the regular Army and was in his third year in the Army reserves when the disease hit) to a 125-pound, emaciated (think Somalia refugee), see-every-bone skeleton who couldn't even get out of his own way or out of his recliner by himself; a man who just the summer before was working out daily and running mile upon mile with his Wilmington, North Carolina, unit and driving heavy equipment for Old Castle Lawn and Garden in Fayetteville, North Carolina. It was a devastating half year for me, my wife, and Scott's only sibling, his sister Marnie. After the funeral we decided as a family that we needed to get away, be away from the parsonage of the Emmanuel Baptist Church in Ellsworth, Maine, where Scott had passed away on an early Saturday morning on April 1, 2017. It felt like a bitter April fool's joke! For our retreat, refuge, and rest my brother Michael offered us the use of his cottage on the Jersey shore, and my wife and I and my daughter's family from California quickly took Michael up on his wonderful gift. It was during that week (we spent the other two weeks with Marnie, her husband Josue, and our only grandchild, a boy named Judah, at their home in Salinas, just a few miles from Monterey Bay, by another sea) on Long Beach Island, one of the barrier islands off the east coast of New Jersey, I once again learned why God made the "seas" (Genesis 1:10). It brought back the times I had spent by a sea over my 66

INTRODUCTION

years, and it is my hope and prayer that these short sermonettes will help you through a painful period in your life, by a sea or no sea.

Jesus often walked by the sea (Matthew 4:18), and He was known to preach and teach by the sea (Luke 5:3). The minute I walked down onto the 22-mile long beach in New Jersey I realized why my brother had fallen in love with the island and had eventually built a cottage there. The air was refreshing (a crisp, clear windy day), the surf was therapeutic, and the sand was empty of humanity except for one lone surf fisherman and another walker like me. It was a place a person could clear his head, think about the past, and reconnect with the Creator of sea and surf. I needed to reconnect because the last six months had tested my faith, my understanding of my Lord, and why His will was to take my son at such an early age. Void of distractions, empty of conflicts, and with time to ponder and meditate on the word of God, I took the time to hear from the sea and the scriptures at the same time. In my quiet, solitary strolls along Long Beach I heard again "a still small voice" (I Kings 19:12), a voice I had often heard when life turns its self upside down. Everybody now and then needs "bit of beach" to calm their nerves, clear their head, and sooth their soul. Over the years I have travelled around the world from Australia to Israel to India, and to countless places in our wonderful fifty states. I haven't always found a sandy surf, but I have discovered enough to write this book. They will be short, sweet, and to the point sermonettes, lessons I have learned from dipping my feet in the various seas my precious Saviour created to help me during troubling times. Long Beach was only the latest. So take off your shoes, let the sand fill the cracks between your toes, lift your eyes toward the sea, open your ears to the sound of the surf, and "be still, and know that I am God" (Psalm 46:10). What does God want to say?

1.

SEA SOVEREIGN

Every sea where I have walked on the beach was created by the Almighty. "And when they heard that, they lifted up their voices to God with one accord, and said, Lord, Thou art God, which hast made heaven, and earth, and THE SEA, and all that in them is." (Acts 4:24) What the early Church proclaimed, I believe. The mighty sea was not an evolutionary afterthought, a chance happening, or a circumstance of nature. I don't believe in chance or circumstance, especially with something that is as mighty as the sea. A Divine Designer following a divine design created the sea, and every time I walk beside a section of it I am reminded of my blessed Creator, much like that first morning (April 18, 2017) on Long Beach in LoveLadies, New Jersey.

The gulls were tapping into the wind currents coming off the Atlantic Ocean as they soared along the surf edge looking for breakfast. Their loud cries could be heard above the pounding surf as their white plumage was ruffled by the mid-April breezes. A small flock of sand darters walked ahead of me scurrying in and out of the surf pecking away as they darted here then there seeking a beach breakfast of their own. Occasionally the tide would get a bit close so the tiny birds would take to flight. It seemed as if one flew, they all flew, but not far, just down the beach a ways, and there they started again their unending, continual searching for a scrap of food the waves might deposit on shore. As I looked up the beach and then back down the beach the way I had come, I could only see a few other individuals wandering as I was, but far enough away to make me believe I had Long Beach all to myself. It was then a deep, abiding peace swept over my spirit. I had felt this kind of peace before on the beaches of Florida, India, California, and Israel. When you go through the death of a child, peace isn't something that comes regularly or easily. Trauma and turmoil are more often the feelings one feels, but despite the roughness of the sea and the roaring of the waves, there is a profound solitude that comes from an isolate strain of sand by a sightless sea.

I deliberately walked as close to the sea edge as I could without getting my feet wet. I wanted to be as close to the grandeur of the water as it lapped in rhythmic order against the sandy beach. All the sounds of the city behind the duns were erased. I heard no human voice, no barking dog, and no laughing kids. My brother told me I would like Long Beach in April because it was crowd less, void of humanity. In the summer the beach was packed, but in the cool of an April week few ventured onto the beach let alone onto the island. So everywhere I looked, I alone saw the splendor of the surf, the beauty of the beach, and diagram of the duns. The loveliness and loneliness of God's divine design relayed to my conscientiousness the goodness and grandeur of my God!

It is in such moments of inspiration and interlude that one realizes the Father does know best, even when that best is a period of separation from your beloved son as the Almighty Himself also experienced (Matthew 27:46). When one looks out into the vastness of the Atlantic Ocean, void of anything (though for a few brief moments I did see a passing cargo ship) yet filled with the majesty and might of the eternal God, one feels so small beside the sea. But are we any bigger beside God? It is on walks like this we get an insight into the working of the Father. If He created the sea (and I believe He did) and if He created Scott (and I believe He did), then He has the right to use either to His honor and glory, and according to Paul to our "good" (Romans 8:28). That first walk on Long Beach went a long way in settling my troubled spirit and traumatized soul.

2.

SEASIDE SERMONS

Some might find it strange my love of the sea and the draw I feel to the ocean, any ocean (I have been to the Pacific, Atlantic, and Indian Oceans). I was raised in landlocked northern Maine, I have a wonderful affection for any course by a beach, and I get terribly sea sick on any boat.

Raised on a potato/dairy farm in Maine's northern most county (Aroostook), I was in my thirties before I spent any time near a sea. In actuality, it wasn't until I moved to an island off the downeast coast of Maine that I began to hear God's sermons from the surf, God's sermonettes by the shore, or God's sermonizing through the sea. It was only then that I understood these words from the pen of Mark: "And He (Jesus) began again to teach by the sea side: and there was gathered unto Him a great multitude, so that He entered into a ship, and sat in the sea; and the whole multitude was by the sea on the land. And he taught them many things by parables, and said unto them in His doctrine" (Mark 4:1-2). In a sun-kissed strand of sand on the shores of the Sea of Galilee Jesus shared with His congregation. On that day in the sea, in the sun, on the sand, and in the surf Jesus shared one of his most famous parables, the sower and the seed (Mark 4:3-20).

There are times when the Almighty will not use the Bible to talk to us, but will use His creation: "The heavens declare the glory of God; and the firmament sheweth His handiwork" (Psalm 19:1). I learned at a very early age from my father to look and listen for God in nature (Job 12:7-9), but in my boyhood those heavens and that firmament were made up of fields and forest, hills and hallows, northern lights and nor-easters. I loved to take long walks through grass, leaves, and soil. Walking along a sea edge was as foreign to me as walking on the moon. Mine was a world of birds and butterflies, dogs and dandelions, cows and chickens. I knew a lot of dry land (Genesis 1:9), but nothing about seas (Genesis 1:10). That is until I moved to Moose Island, a small island in Passamaquoddy Bay in Maine's eastern most county, Washington, and the Washington Street Baptist Church in Eastport, Maine.

For five years I lived on that rock-bound island and it was there I fell in love with the sea and learned to listen to the lessons of a wintry storm in a watery bay. In the pounding surf I heard the stormy voice of God. In the howling of the ocean wind I heard the undertones of God. In the rise and fall of the twenty-foot tides I heard the still small voice of God. It was there I got a chance to walk the seashore and watch the awesomeness of the Almighty unfold with each changing tide. It was not the first time I had been near the ocean because in 1972 I dipped my feet in the seas off Melbourne, Australia. I had played a number of times in the beaches of southern Maine, but it wasn't until I strolled Greenlaw Beach that I discovered God's sea sermons. Over sixty months I watched the faithful rise and fall of the tides, and I found again the faithfulness of God (II Timothy 2:13). The inlets and coves around Moose Island and its many beaches highlighted for me again and underlined for me again the mighty God that I was serving.

As I recall the past and remember other trips to God's shoreline, Long Beach is just the latest as I also remember Casperson Beach in Florida, Eve's Beach in Kerala, Caesarea Beach in Israel, Huntington Beach in California, Herring Beach in Canada, and Old Orchard Beach in Maine. It is my prayer that these sermonettes will last longer than the footprints in the sand I left as I walked with God by the seashores of my life.

3.

SOUTHERN SEA

The news from 262 Flinders Lane (the location of the United Aborigines Mission in Melbourne, Australia) was disappointing. We had been accepted as summer missionaries for ministries in Western Australia, but a train strike delayed our departure to a place called Cosmo Newbery. So now what? It was then Bob and I learned it is not "now what?" But "now wait!" It was then we also learned that *you can do a whole lot for the Lord while you are waiting upon the Lord.* (My cousin Bob Blackstone and I were in Australia on a 68-day short-term mission's trip in the summer of 1972. We had arrived in eastern Australia with only one contact and that contact had directed us to a mission that worked with aboriginals in the western part of the country. While waiting for a cross-country train ride, I first learned what a trip to the sea can do for a doubting spirit.)

After the stress and strain of our last few months at collage (my junior year and Bob's sophomore year at Bob Jones University in Greenville, South Carolina), the added pressure of planning a summer mission trip to Australia (our first time out of the United States), and the jet lag of flying halfway around the world (literally half-way around the world from the northern hemisphere to the southern hemisphere), the good Lord knew we needed a bit of rest before we faced the harsh conditions of the Gibson Desert. So He allowed us ten beautiful days in Melbourne ministering and being ministered to by some very godly people. We had hardly hit the ground when we were taken to a youth camp by the sea called Mayfield where we became counselors to a group of Australian young adults. One of the first postcards I sent home was to my girlfriend and future wife, Coleen. This is what I wrote about Mayfield: "I thought I would get a few postcards off to the folks. Tell your folks I will try to get one off to them, but I have run out of them and we are out-of-touch with the city now. We are working at a camp by the sea. It is a youth camp. I have a cabin of five guys mostly my age. We have had a great time. Mr. Garlock (Frank Garlock, the founder of Majesty Music and a teacher at Bob Jones at the time, was in Melbourne, unbeknownst to us. You can imagine Bob's and my surprise when we walked into the chapel and saw a familiar face) spoke last night. He is going to be here today and tonight and is showing "Gateway to a Miracle" [Bob Jones' promotion film at the time]. So it is a little BJU here this weekend. We went out touring yesterday; saw some great country; got some good pictures. I wanted you to know that I wrote our names in the sands of the Pacific. I did this on a beach at the southern-most point of Australia!"

The weekend Bob and I spent in a camp by the ocean allowed us to "mount up" and soar for the rest of the summer, just like Isaiah promised: "But they that wait upon the Lord shall renew their strength; they shall mount up with wings as eagles; they shall run and not be weary; they shall walk and not faint." (Isaiah 40:31) The verse was our society verse. Both Bob and I belonged to Basilean, a boys' society at Bob Jones University. At every meeting we would quote Isaiah 40:31 so by the time Bob and I got stranded in Melbourne, we knew it by heart. But it was in Melbourne that it got into our hearts. And it was on a beach in Melbourne I came to understand that like Asher (Judges 5:17) we are not to continue ". . . on the sea shore . . . ," but only use the seashore for a place of rest, recovery, and renewal for the ministry before us. I did that on my first seaside visit and every seaside visit since including the one I took to Long Beach, New Jersey, to refocus since the passing of my son, Scott. Seashores are not for residing but for restoring.

4.

KOVALAM, KERALA

Russ Coffin, a deacon of the Emmanuel Baptist Church and myself went on a short-term mission's trip to India to dedicate a sanctuary and a parsonage built by funds given by the people of our assembly in Ellsworth, Maine. The second full day in India was divided between tourist things and ministry things. India has always been full of surprises for me. Despite the advance schedule sent to me by Shibu Simon (president of the India ministry), I was immediately surprised when Shaju Simon (his brother) told us that we would be staying in the Trivandrum (where we flew into) area for our first weekend in Kerala. Once I realized we were not heading directly to Kangazha (home town of the India ministry Emmanuel had been supporting for over a decade), I began to understand just how the good Lord was answering one of my India prayers (finishing visiting all the churches of the IGBC, Independent Gospel Baptist Church of India) and at the same time bring Russ face to face with a man he had personally helped.

Because our first service wasn't until that evening, Binu (our driver) and Shaju had time to show us around Trivandrum, the biggest city in Kerala State. I had traveled in and out of Trivandrum four times, but hadn't stayed in the city for long. After a breakfast of eggs, English toast, pomegranates, and bananas, we headed off to Kovalam Beach to introduce Russ to the Indian Ocean. The fifteen mile trip took us about an hour, but the trip was worth every minute to me. This would be my third visit to the best beach in the world, at least according to me. (When I wrote this article

I had not visited Long Beach and Huntington Beach so maybe Kovalam Beach isn't as far up on my top ten beaches as it used to be.) I had fallen in love with this pleasant coastline on my first trip (2006) and had brought my daughter (Marnie) back to this white-sandy shore a year later. I wanted Russ to experience the warm water, the hot sand, and the cooler breezes before the heat and humidity of the inland overwhelmed him, and to show him that there was one place in India that would remind him of his beloved coastline of Maine. I wanted Russ to taste the salty air from the Arabian Sea, taste the salty peanuts from the local vendors, and feel the relief that comes to your sandal-sore feet as you walked through the salty sand and wade in the salty sea. There is no greater place to begin a spiritual adventure than on a beach to which the Psalmist described by writing "... this great and wide sea ..." (Psalm 104:25)

Our stroll along Eve's Beach (another beach attached to Kovalam), our picture in front of Kovalam Lighthouse, one of the greatest lighthouse I have seen (Long Beach also has a lighthouse at the northern end of it called Barnegat), and our wading into the high surf was all I had expected and hoped for when after an hour we headed back into town. Russ was the first to spot the lumbering giant walking up a side lane near the road we were traveling. Russ was excited to seen the elephant and its trainer in heavy, big-city traffic, something you would never see in Ellsworth. That Saturday night Russ and I visited with the saints at the Narani and Ooruttambalam Baptist Churches, both pastored by T. P. Sachai. I had a chance in 2007 to visit the Ooruttambalam Church and the home of Pastor Sachai and his wife with my daughter Marnie. I had their son Libin in my classes at Kerala Baptist Bible College in 2006. The highlight of the evening was for Russ to meet Pastor Sachai and his bike. In 2009 Russ headed up a fund raising endeavor to buy Pastor Sachai a motorcycle. Now Russ was able to shake hands with and speak face to face with a man he had helped in his ministry for nearly two years now, and to fulfill Paul's precept of "for we are labourers together with God..." (I Corinthians 3:9), even when you are a half a world apart! From beaches to blessings, a day doesn't get any better than that.

5.

MEDITERRANEAN MASTERPIECE

Just before ten o'clock our bus, with Joel at the wheel, pulled into Caesarea National Park, the archaeological remains of Herod the Great's amazing seaport. My daughter Marnie and I were on a tour of Israel through Dallas Theological Seminary in May of 2010 when we got a chance to explore this Mediterranean masterpiece.

I had been impressed with Herod's temple mount in Jerusalem, and his forts at the Herodium and Masada had also wowed me, but I was not ready for the sheer size of the work when we explored the elaborate complex of Caesarea. Herod knew there was money to be made if he could tap into the trade routes of Roman Empire. He had a monopoly on a variety of products wanted by the Romans, but how was he to get the products to them? If he had his own seaport, he could cut out the middle man and deal directly with markets around the Mediterranean Sea. If Herod could build a hill where there had previously been no hill and place a palace fortress on its top, he could also build a port where there had never been a port and create a very unique breakwater to protect it. As he did so many times before in his long reign, about 22 BC Herod told his engineers and builders to create a seaport about half way between Joppa (II Chronicles 2:16) and Dora (Dor-I Chronicles 7:29) in honor of Octavian Augustus Caesar, his patron at the time. Because this seaport was located about 50 miles northwest of Jerusalem on the vital Egypt to the Tyre (the great seaport in Lebanon) road, Caesarea would within Herod's lifetime dominate Israel's sea trade.

What makes Caesarea so special for me was its location on a beach. Ever since I first moved to the coast of Maine in 1986 (I have now lived over half my life near the ocean), I have fallen in love with the sea. Caesarea was for me one of the most beautiful spots in all of Israel. Despite the ruins and rubble, I enjoyed our three hour walk around this coastal city because of the sea breezes, the ocean sights, and the water vista. Our trip through Caesarea took us through the theatre (seating capacity of 4000), Herod's promontory palace (a group of half-submerged walls are all that is left of the fabled palace), a hippodrome, one of the largest in the Roman Empire (the massive stones that remain allow you to imagine its former size), the Roman and Byzantine streets through the commercial and administrative area, the bathhouse complex, the harbor (still surrounded by walls dating back to 1250), the old medieval fortified city, the temple platform, statues square (all kinds of ancients statues, tombs, and pillars), the synagogue, and finally out through the Byzantine gate and walls, and all with an ocean side view and with beach front access. It doesn't get any better than that!

For me to imagine that I might have walked on stones that Philip (Acts 8:40), Peter (Acts 10:6, 24), or Paul (Acts 23:33) might have walked on was enough for me. To see the expansive stones and the imaginative breakwater which formed a large artificial harbor (Sebastos) using the 1200 foot breakwater as the base for the inner quay and anchorage area of mooring stones and the simple architecture was breathtaking. I caught myself more than once thinking of how the eternal God moved a wicked king to create an elaborate port, not for the export of goods, but for the export of the Gospel. The more I saw the world of Jesus through the archaeological sites, the more I understood Paul's statement: "When the fullness of time was come, God sent forth His son . . ." (Galatians 4:4) I had been taught that history was waiting for the Greek language to be in place, the Roman road system to be built, the Pax Romana (worldwide peace) to be in effect, and now I know for a harbor to be constructed on the Mediterranean Sea.

6.

AMAZING AQUEDUCT

To my sheer delight our stay at Caesarea by the sea didn't stop with a tour around the ruins of that ancient seaport. We exited Caesarea through the eastern wall (a perimeter wall nearly a mile and a half around) gate of the old Byzantine section of the town. The gate contained an impressive tower and the moat was spectacular, the best I had ever seen including some memorable moats my wife and I had seen on our trip to England, Scotland, and Wales in 2003. As Joel drove away from the city limits of Caesarea, Greg pointed out the old Roman amphitheatre dating back to the second century, an arena where gladiatorial and animal combat was waged. On the other side of the road a massive hippodrome (circus), also of the second century and Roman, was being uncovered. The structure was nearly 1500 feet long and 300 feet wide. They believe it could seat 30,000 spectators to the races. A series of columns set along the wall through the middle of the race track have been uncovered as well as a 75-foot obelisk. It was only an introduction to what was coming next as we drove up the Mediterranean coast.

I had seen pictures and had dreamed many times of visiting the most recognizable artifact of Caesarea, the high-level aqueduct. This marvel of ancient engineering still runs along an exposed beach just north of the city. Since Caesarea had no natural rivers or springs nearby to supply the drinking water for this important center, something had to be done. Because this city (Caesarea was the home of the Roman procurators, including Pontius

Pilate whose name, interestingly, was discovered in Caesarea on an inscription naming him "the prefect of Judah.") was a seat of the Roman government for the region for 500 years, the water system was started by Herod the Great and modified by the Romans. An aqueduct is a water carrying system where water is transported from one area to another by a series of canals. Because gravity was the means of powering this system in low laying areas, that section of the aqueduct is carried on arches. It was to a section of those arches we stopped to examine this amazing accomplishment. I had read about such structures for years, but had only visited one such place in my life, a relatively modern aqueduct system at Llangollen, Wales. This 46-mile-long canal which only drops one inch per mile also contains the tallest navigable aqueduct in England. My wife and I were thrilled to have floated across this 126-foot-high aqueduct in a narrowboat in our 2003 trip. The day I was in Wales, I never imagined I was going to get a chance to experience a nearly 2000 year old aqueduct on the Mediterranean Sea.

We stopped where the old aqueduct now comes to an end. Time had certainly taken its toll on the arches and canals. We could hardly imagine this structure running to the Shuni springs at the base of Mount Carmel nearly 15 miles to our north. I was told that along the route water from the Crocodile River (a small culvert carried water from an artificial reservoir that was formed with the damming of the river) was also added to the flow, and that on the way a tunnel had to be hewn through the Kurkar Ridge. Where we stopped the aqueduct stood a good 25 feet over the beach, a perfect picture-taking spot. Marnie and I got our pictures taken under the arch and by the aqueduct as we enjoyed the refreshing sea breeze. As I did at Caesarea, I walked the seashore to get an ocean side look at the conduit. We could only stay at the aqueduct for a few minutes because our schedule had us exploring Mount Carmel before dark. Again the visit was cut short in my opinion, but a few minutes were better than no minutes at all. Such is the joy of any minutes on a sandy beach by a sea shore, aqueduct or no aqueduct.

7.

WAVE WISDOM

On a recent trip to Sarasota, Florida, I had the sheer joy of walking on two separate beaches along the Gulf of Mexico. It was my first visit to the Sunshine State, and I must admit I had never had a desire to visit this southern paradise before, but now I am grateful for the opportunity to have explored this sandy corner of beach and learn this marvellous precept from the Psalmist: "Which stilleth the noise of the sea, the noise of their waves, and the tumult of the people." (Psalm 65:7)

The idea for this beach vacation actually came from our church family at the Emmanuel Baptist Church. As a Thanksgiving gift to my wife and me for seven years (we have been there 28 years now) of service, they gave us an all-expense paid, nine-day trip to sunny Florida in the middle of a cold January in Maine. We left Maine with the temperature at twenty and arrived in Florida with the temperature at seventy. I thought I was leaving winter for spring, but found we had advanced into summer. The grass was green, the birds were singing, and the winds were warm. What a change!

Two of the highlights of this surprise adventure into a warmer climate were Casperson Beach and Nokomis Beach. I hadn't walked on such beaches in my fifty years on this planet. Oh, I had walked on plenty of beaches, but nothing like these two sandy shores. The sand was warm, the water was warm (though most of the people that shared these beaches with us thought it was still too cold), and the sun was warm. Two of the reasons I never desired to visit Florida were "hot and humid." I had spent four years of my life in Greenville, South Carolina, attending a Bible school, and I never enjoyed the weather because even though I never stayed for the summer, it was still too hot and humid for me. So my conclusion was if I travelled further south, the weather would be muggier and much hotter. But in mid-January 1999 along the Gulf Coast, the weather was warm enough to stroll in the surf and swim in the sea which was ideal.

I enjoyed Casperson Beach because it was my first experience strolling on sand in the winter. We collected shark's teeth along the shore and basked in the sun's rays. Despite the direct light, the sea breeze kept us refreshed. On the last day of our vacation, we went to Nokomis Beach just a short distance from where we were staying. At Casperson Beach, the sea was calm with hardly a wave on the bright blue sea. At Nokomis, a few days later, the ocean was still boiling after a powerful storm had blown through the day before. The sea was rolling and the waves were crashing onto the beach with great force. It was then I came to the conclusion that I really enjoyed high surf over calm seas.

As I stood in the surf and took the patterned blows of the walls of water rolling in from the Mexican Gulf, I meditated on the phenomenon of the waves produced by the sun and storm. Born hundreds of miles out into the Gulf, I watched in awe and wonder as they splashed in the sun for a moment and then kissed the beaches at Nokomis. I felt their tremendous strength as they literally picked me up and flung me towards shore. The waves, perhaps more than any other part of the ocean, remind me of the invisible, but powerful hand of our heavenly Father. The Psalmist was right when he wrote about the stilling of the sea. Despite the cry of the seagulls and sand pipers and the rumbling of the waves, for a few fleeting moments in the rising surf on Nokomis Beach my soul was perfectly still, and there was no tumult in my spirit. How is it that in the midst of a storm tossed sea one can find such tranquility and solitude? The answer is the One that "stilleth . . . !"

8.

MIGHTY MYSTERY

I had gone for a walk at the ocean's edge after a heavy storm had passed over Passamaquoddy Bay, the bay that surrounds the coastal community of Eastport where I was a pastor. I discovered on similar walks that in order to hear the "still small voice" of God, you must stroll in quiet awe and humble grace to understand the mighty mystery of the sea.

The seas of the earth are a mighty mass of water covering three-quarters of this planet's surface. Because of the vast volume, man, despite thousands of years, barely understands the basic elements that govern this vast part of our world. Within the depths of this colossus huge currents flow (rivers greater than the Amazon or the Nile), and on its surface rides enormous waves created by the power of the sun and the energy of the wind. Man has discovered the magnetic attraction of the moon and the sun and the other planets of our solar system, but still hasn't grasp the truth of another Power that rules the waves and commands the tides and holds them all in check: "But the heavens and the earth, which are now, by the same word are kept in store . . ." (II Peter 3:7) Years before Peter wrote, the Psalmist knew of the unseen power and the unheard voice that commands and controls this enormously complex and complicated corner of our world. "When He gave to the sea His decree, that the waters should not pass His commandments: when he appointed the foundations of the earth." (Proverbs 8:29)

During my years on an island off the downeast coast of Maine, the ups and downs of the tide upon the beaches surrounding Moose Island were a constant reminder that my heavenly Father was the God of order and time. Even the mighty oceans obey His clock. All it would take is an honest man watching the tides to conclude that it is not by mere chance or circumstance that a combination of stars, sun, and moon affect the ocean tides, the surf, and the sea. It is for this reason I love to walk the beaches of the world. Whether walking along the breakwater in Eastport during a powerful winter storm or the shoreline of Greenlaw Beach during "a lazy, hazy day of summer," the ocean is a constant reminder to me just how massive, how mighty, and how mysterious my God is.

Yes, like the sea, God is still a mighty mystery to me. Yet, each time I return from the Oceanside, I seem to understand a bit more of who my Lord and Saviour really is. I see in the sand along the shore His brilliant artistry, and just as each wave wipes clean the beach for another clean canvas to walk upon, so it is what happens when He forgives my sins. Despite countless footprints, missteps, detours, and diversions, the power of the surf erases all marks, just like the blood of Jesus Christ (Ephesians 1:7). Despite countless footprints of sin on our life, one wave of confession (I John 1:9) will wash the soul as white as the sand on Nokomis Beach in Florida, or Greenlaw Beach in Eastport, or Eve's Beach in Kovalam. Yes, even whiter than snow (Isaiah 1:18).

I would be the first to say that I know very little of the seas. Even after a lifetime studying the Bible I would be the first to say I know very little of the cleansing power of the blood of Christ. I have made relatively few journeys to the sea's edge, but I have made many journeys to God's throne (shore) of grace (Hebrews 4:16) to ask forgiveness for a transgression or iniquity that I have done and have always found forgiveness. Permeating every rise and fall of an Eastport tide, engulfing every wave that strikes the Maine shore, and embodied in every drop of water in Passamaquoddy Bay is the undeniable, debatable truth that the Creator God controls and commands it all, and He also controls and commands all sins will be forgiven if exposed to the Blood (I John 1:7).

9.

SOUTHERN SOUNDS

My devotional reading for the year 1999 was W. Phillip Keller's book "Songs of the Soul." Keller is most famous for his classic book on "A Shepherd Looks at Psalm 23." A missionary's son who was raised in the wilds of Africa, Keller would go on to become a well-respected naturalist, writer, and "a man of God." I have enjoyed his books, having now read most of them. I think the reason I like his writings is the subject matter of his books. Often as I read his insights and observations I recall a similar experience, maybe not in the same place, but a similar encounter. A case in point is something that happened to me while on vacation on the beaches of western Florida.

Just before I took a trip with my wife Coleen to the gulf side of Florida, I read this on January 11, 1999, under Keller's title, "The Sound of the Surf." Little did I know that in just a few short days I would experience what Keller was writing about. "A large part of the unalloyed fascination of the seashore is the symphonic variation of the melodies played upon it. There are days when the sea, under a brittle blue summer sky, [it was a winter sky I found in Florida, but being from Maine, it felt like summer to me] barely whispers in a soft notes of tiny wavelets caressing the sand . . . like the gentle tone of a violin string section. [I heard those violins on Casperson Beach in Venice, Florida, and I have heard those same violins on beaches from Israel to India.] Other days there is the steady beat of breakers pounding the rocks like drums in the distance? Then there are times when with thundering notes there are the trumpet sounds of great waves rolling in from the deeps-the crash of their breakers on the beach like the clash of cymbals in the hands of the celestial music Maker. [I heard those cymbals at Nokomis Beach on Casey Key, and I have heard those sounds in the crashing of the surf on Sandy Beach in Acadia National Park, Maine's most famous national park.] In all of this I find enormous stimulation, splendor, and joy. The sound of the surf speaks to me at the greatest depth of my being. It is ever there, ever present, ever pervasive. Even though my thoughts and emotions may be preoccupied with other interests and activities, in the background there persists the eternal song of the sea. Just so, our Heavenly Father speaks to us in myriad ways as we live out our little lives in fellowship with Him. Sometimes His voice comes as loudly as the sound of thunder on a sultry summer night. [I also listened one night to such a southern storm roar over us on our Florida adventure.] At other times His voice is as soft and subtle as a gentle summer breeze. [Each night my wife and I would walk the park we were staying in and hear that sound, a 'still small voice' kind of a sound.] I must listen quietly and closely or I may miss the blessing He has for me."

What I learned in my Florida trip through the message of Keller's devotional was that whether in Maine during a great "nor-easter" or in the Sunshine State during a severe thunder and lightning storm, my God is to be listened to. Whether a dead calm sea or a roaring ocean, my God's voice can be heard. I found this in one of the Psalms: "Let the sea roar, and the fulness thereof; the world, and they that dwell therein." (Psalm 98:7) My venue may change; the topography may be different, as well as the State, but God is still speaking, sometimes loud and clear and sometimes mysterious and unclear. His messages might change and the tone of His voice might change, but whether in "the sound of the surf" or in "a still small voice," He is speaking. He might use the sound of a sparrow in a southern pine or the sound of a storm over a silent sea, but, let us be clear about this, He is speaking. The Father speaks in sounds we do understand, but are we listening?

10.

VIOLENT VOICES

I have a tape I play sometimes just before I go to sleep at night of nothing but the sounds of running water. Whether a babbling brook, a rippling river, a cascading creek, or an oscillating ocean, my soul is quieted by the different voices of moving water. The simple sounds of a Maine stream moving through a hardwood forest brought a silent serenity to my spirit as a boy, as did the peaceful noise of a Canadian river moving majestically after ice-out brought solitude to my soul as an adult. Now in my old age (just turned 66 and my first Social Security checks have been deposited in my bank) it seems to be the sound of the sea that brings tranquility to both my physical being and my eternal being. Sooner or later, and I am glad I started early, most will instinctively be drawn to the relaxing voices of free-flowing waters, whether over rocks and reef, sand, or shore.

Despite my early years of being drawn to singing streams, in my latter years I am being led to the surging seas. Unlike its weaker relatives, the sea contains the ability of extremes of expression. Also in my collection of natural sound tapes one is just the noises of waves splashing and lapping on shore. What is it about these sounds, water flowing over rocks, water falling from great heights, or water over riding sand that brings such pleasantness to our minds, bodies, and emotions? It doesn't seem to make any difference whether the sound is soft or violent. It affects us in a deep spiritual way. I have walked along the seashore when the water could barely be heard. All that was heard was the seagulls fighting for a small bit of shrimp being washed up on shore by the rising tides and sea surf. But there have been times during my stroll along the seashore that only the sea could be heard. The seagulls are still even though they are chattering away at each other, but their beaks only move because their voice is being drowned out by the roar of the ocean. If I learned anything in my years on the coast of Maine, it is just how loud the sea can be, and not just loud but violently loud!

Jeremiah spoke of this violent voice in Jeremiah 6:23: "They shall lay hold on the bow and spear; they are cruel, and have no mercy; *their voice roareth like the sea*; and they ride upon horses, set in array as men for war against thee, O daughters of Zion." Jeremiah was speaking of the violence of an advancing army, and the cruelty and lack of mercy of a conquering warrior. In the middle he likens their sound to the roar of a sea. Can the sea get angry? Can the ocean turn violent? I personally love a quieter sea, a gentle ocean, but there is a draw for me when I hear a bellowing sea just as long as I am not upon it and can witness it from afar. I have heard the roar Jeremiah writes about. It is then the sun worshippers' move inland and the beachcombers move off island. At the height of the sea storm only a few remain because everybody knows what an angry ocean can do especially when kicked up by winds like a hurricane Sandy. While walking Long Beach I met a man who reminded me of hurricane Sandy. I was actually in India on my fourth trip to the subcontinent when I had to stay in Kerala two extra days because they were not allowing anybody to fly into JFK. The man on the beach told me of the damage to his property, the aftermath of a violent voice.

I have heard that violent voice roaring over Moose Island. It is a voice that overwhelms any human sound, natural or created. It is loud and haunting, and yes, terrifying at times. If one doesn't respect such a voice, trouble will find them like the mariners of old found out. For those who disobey the warning voice of the sea will disobey at their own peril. So too must we respect the warning voice of God.

11.

SEASHORE SUNSET

We were in a hurry because we still had 17 miles to travel to fulfill Marnie's last desire for this trip. My daughter Marnie and I were at the end of a 17-day, short-term mission's trip to Kerala, India, where I had been graduation speaker for the closing programs of the 2006-2007 school year at Kerala Baptist Bible College. Marnie loves the ocean, any ocean, and she wanted to dip her feet in the Indian Ocean before we headed home to Maine (when we got back home Marnie would apply and be accepted for a Master's Program through Dallas Theological Seminary in Texas). She also loves sunsets, and she wanted to see the sun set over the Indian Ocean. I had told her of my adventure in the Indian Ocean the year before, and she wanted to experience the thrill for herself. Binu, our driver, somehow managed to weave his way through rush hour traffic so by a little after five o'clock we were standing in the sands of Kovalam Beach.

For the next hour and a half, I watched Shibu, Shaju, Binu, Joshua (Shibu's son), and Marnie play like children in the heavy, pounding surf. The boys (I call them boys because they are the same age as my son) had brought me to the same beach a little over a year before, but there was something different about this time. I saw a family at play, swimming, body surfing, building sand castles, buying roasted peanuts from the beach vendors, and watching together a spectacular Indian sunset over Kovalam Cove. Marnie and Binu (as with any father I had my favorites of Marnie's boyfriends as she grew up and Binu was husband material) were like best friends as they created Edayappara (the village where Kerala Baptist Bible College is located) in the sands of Kovalam. I walked from one end of the beach to the other enjoying the refreshing and much cooler air, the best of the trip. I took pictures and prayed that this wasn't my last trip to Kerala (and it wasn't because I would return in 2010, 2012, and again in 2016). I had fallen in love with this place and its people all over again, and my beach stroll was only the cherry on the top of my Indian Sunday!

One of the side benefits of a seashore is the unobstructed view of a setting sun, a sun that seems bigger on a beach and a sun that seemingly disappears into the ocean as it goes down. Our time in Kerala was drawing to a close, but we still had enough time to wait on shore for the setting of the sun. One of my favorite pictures of my Indian adventures is a picture Shibu took of Marnie and me with Eve's Beach behind us and behind Eve's Beach the last sliver of the sun dipping into the distant horizon. The gusty wind had weakened to a slight breeze. The warm air had turned a bit cooler. The flocks of people that had shared the beach with us during the last hours of the afternoon had departed. Only a few diehards remained with a few beach vendors. For us the shoreline off Kovalam had become a sanctuary, and God was preaching a sermon to me. I was reminded of this phrase from one of the verses of the Book of Joshua: ". . . And unto the great sea toward the going down of the sun . . ." (Joshua 1:4) Granted, God was speaking about the Mediterranean Sea and not the Indian Ocean, but He was speaking about the same sun. This scene can't shape itself, but is the result of the Almighty Hand. Just like Kovalam Beach or the sandy coves around the inlet to this Kerala coastline didn't shape itself, neither can man shape himself. The self-made-man is a worldly falsehood.

As the hot sun dipped into the Indian Ocean, we watched in amazement as one of the great sights of nature took place before our eyes. Whether the coast of Maine or the coast of Kerala, a sunset isn't an ending or a goodbye, but just an anticipation of another day spent with family and friends on the shorelines of life waiting our next sunset.

12.

SOLID SEA

W. Phillip Keller wrote this comment to I Samuel 2:8: "For the foundations of the earth are the Lord's; upon them He has set the world." (New International Version) "There is in the ocean a remarkable bond that encircles the entire globe. Its waters, though arbitrarily divided by man into separate seas, are really one. This flowing water, which is ever in flux, covers roughly three-quarters of the planet. It is in no sense static or stagnant. It is eternally active, ever in motion, relentlessly flowing with formable force in great ocean currents. Yet it binds and unites all of the earth in a single unit. The oceans encircle, touch, and caress every continent, every land mass, every island, and every rock that protrudes from the sea floor. The ocean has this great glory of unifying the globe, shaping its coasts, tempering its climate, and general contributing to the total environment in which life survives and thrives. I can never stand-alone high on a sea cliff, with the ocean roaring on the rocks below me, and not sense an overwhelming wave of genuine gratitude sweep through my spirit. There engulfs me the simultaneous sensations of my own insignificance and the glorious grandeur of the entire globe of which I am a minute part. There is imparted to me during these quiet interludes the indelible, irrefutable impression that 'This is my Father's world.'"

I still remember the first time I came to this same conclusion. I was flying over the Pacific Ocean on my way to Australia for a short-term, summer ministry among the Aboriginals of Western Australia. The South

Sea seemed to never end as we flew from Honolulu, Hawaii, to Sydney, Australia. The second time I had that feeling was when I looked over that same solid sea just south of Melbourne. We had to stay in Melbourne for an extra week because of a national train strike. While we were there my cousin Bob, my companion for this spiritual and natural adventure, and I were taken to a high cliff overlooking the Bass Straights between Australia and Tasmania. Being a landlock, farmer's son from northern Maine, it was my first flight and first view of the might and mass of the seas. It was my first true glimpse of something forever huge. I thought the hills of my home state were big until I flew over the Rocky Mountains on that trip for the first time. I thought Square Lake in Aroostook County was a large body of water until I flew over the Pacific Ocean. I hadn't even visited the Atlantic Ocean then so during my very first trip away from Maine I discovered just how big the planet was on which I was living. I like Keller came to the same conclusion that this is truly my Father's world.

From childhood I had sung Maltbie Babcock's classic church hymn. It was only after I learned the history of this song did I realize that there were others who also saw the world through spiritual eyes. Dr. Babcock was a Presbyterian minister who loved the out-of-doors. It seems he would say every time he went for his early morning walks, "I'm going out to see my Father's world!" He believed as I do and Keller did, "The earth is the Lord's and the fulness thereof; the world, and they that dwell therein. For He founded it upon the seas, and established it upon the floods." (Psalm 24:1-2) Now we can understand these lines: "This is my Father's world, and to my listening ears all nature sings, and round me sings the music of the spheres. This is my Father's world! I rest me in the thought of rocks and trees, of skies and seas, His hand the wonders wrought." When I was a kid I thought my God was big, but it wasn't until I flew over the Pacific Ocean that I recognized just how big He really is. Seeing the majestic seas and the mighty mountains, I started to realize the mighty, massive, marvelous God I serve!

13.

HERRING HIKE

When it finally hits you that your little girl is no longer a baby, something happens to you as a father. I still remember clearly the event as if it were today when once again the sea and seashore revealed the amazing transformation to my heart.

I was so proud the day my nine-month-old Marnie took her first steps (three months ahead of her brother). This spirited tot was determined to keep pace with her thirty-seven month old brother Scott. I laughed within myself as I watched my daughter grow faster than her years. At the time I thought it was funny, but now I know it wasn't. Granted, I tried at times to slow her down, but her strong will was too much for either her mother or me. Not only did her walking ability quickly catch up to her brother, but her growth was getting close as well. It wasn't long before Coleen and I realized why the good Lord had given Scott a 27-month head start. For a number of years most people thought Marnie and Scott were less than a year apart. That is until Scott turned twelve, and then Marnie never had a chance. What I learned too late was a step quickly becomes a walk, and even more quickly a walk becomes a run. As the days passed rapidly onward, a succession of steps resulted in my cute child being transformed into a grade school girl. We had by that time moved to Moose Island off the downeast coast of Maine where Marnie's steps were widening.

Then it happened. My mother, Phyllis, and my father, Wendell, were down from Aroostook County for a visit, and we decided to show them the sea. We lived just across Passamaquoddy Bay from Campobello Island, Canada, and President Franklin Roosevelt's summer retreat. (You could literally see his house from a bluff on Moose Island just three miles away.) The weather was glorious so we decided to take a picnic lunch and visit the sites of Canada's fabled island. A quick trip down US Route One to Route 189 brought us into the small coastal village of Lubec. We crossed the International Bridge onto Campobello Island and headed straight to Herring Cove on the Atlantic side and the back side of the island for lunch. We would wait on our explorations until we showed Mum and Dad a full view of the ocean. I had never been there before, but some friends told me that the sights were spectacular and the scenery spellbinding.

We were not disappointed as we left the car in the public parking area and made our way to the picnic area by the shore. The rockbound coast was interrupted by a white sand and gravel beach that seemed to stretch up the shoreline for miles. After lunch the kids decided to go near the ocean and look for shells, starfish, and any other treasures they could find in their first beachcombing adventure. It was a clear day so you could see Grand Manan Island in the distance, the only obstruction to the open ocean. Sitting in the middle of the Bay of Fundy, its high white cliffs could be seen despite the twenty miles between Grand Manan Island and Campobello Island. After taking in the grandeur of the view and the grandness of the vista, my eyes refocused on the two children far up the shoreline. I decided to join them, and it was a decision I made that I will never forget for as long as I live.

"Now as he walked by the sea . . ." (Mark 1:10) As I slowly plodded towards my daughter, I experienced flashbacks to the times she only took steps. Now she was walking and running all over Herring Beach. As I approached her she showed me the shells and starfish she had found, and then to my surprise she asked me to take her hand and walk with her. For one of the few times in my life I wished that moment of time could be stopped. It was there on a wind sweep Canadian beach my Mar (Marnie's nickname) turned into a young lady.

14.

TURNING TIDE

It was around 1:30 PM when I headed out of Eastport Harbor for Head Harbor. Our destination was the tip of Campobello Island, Canada, and the rich fishing grounds at the mouth of Passamaquoddy Bay. Our boat captain for the day was Peter Ricker, a dear Christian friend and an expert in catching big Pollack. It was the first day of August and the mainland was experiencing a hot, sticky spell. Even on and around Moose Island it was humid, and the heat created a thick hazy. A heavy, cool wind, however, felt good over the cold waters of the three-mile wide bay. The water temperature in Passamaquoddy Bay barely gets into the mid-50s so despite the rough seas the change in temperature was worth the trip, fish or no fish! The Passamaquoddy air conditioner was working just fine as we passed Todd's Head and made our way across the bay into Canadian waters.

This was my third summer on Moose Island, better known as Eastport, and being our first time living on the coast of Maine I was just getting used to living with the tides. When you live on a piece of land surrounded by ocean water, the tides affect everything from fishing to the weather. Coming onto the island at low tide makes you wonder if it is possible for the numerous empty coves and inlets along the shore to ever be filled again, but before long the mighty and massive Atlantic Ocean fills those same bays with its seemingly endless resources of liquid. Tides of twenty to thirty feet are common along this shoreline from Maine to New Brunswick. Boats nearly resting on the sea floor at noon at the breakwater in Eastport Harbor are rocking peacefully parallel with the piers at supper time. I feel Job must have had "a turning of the tide" experience to write this: "As the waters fail from the sea, and the flood decayeth and drieth up . . . ," (Job 14:11) a perfect description of the tides in Passamaquoddy Bay.

It was on such fishing trips into this ever changing bay with its twice daily risings and ebbing's, I learned of the all-sufficient God. Paul Van Gorder once wrote: "Looking at ourselves, we sometimes see a vast emptiness inside. Perhaps the void is created by sorrow or bereavement. Or maybe it's the result of failure, pride, jealousy, and bitterness. From our hearts we cry out, "Is there enough grace for me?" And then God answers our plea by letting His love flow in upon us like a mighty ocean!" Like the tide of Passamaquoddy Bay, the grace of God fills when we hit the ebb of our lives, the ebb of our experience, or the ebb of our loss. When Paul was empty, hurting, and haunted by ". . . a thorn in his flesh . . ." (II Corinthians 12:7), he heard that still small voice of God say *"My grace is sufficient for thee."* (II Corinthians 12:9) As I first wondered if there could possibly be enough water to fill the coves surrounding Eastport, I soon learned that there was enough and sometimes on a full moon, more. Sometimes I would stand on the shoreline at Greenlaw Beach and watch the tide come in and wonder if it would ever stop. It was on that shoreline that I understood these works from Annie Johnson Flint, words I had been singing since childhood but whose sermon I never fully fathomed until I experienced the turning of the tides on the coast of Maine: "He giveth more grace when the burden grows greater; He sendeth more strength with the labors increase. To added affliction He addeth His mercy; to multiplied trials, His multiplied peace. When we have exhausted our store of endurance, when our strength has failed ere the day is half done, when we reached the end of our hoarded resources, Our Father's full giving is only begun. His love has no limit; His grace has no measure; His power has no boundary known unto men, for out of His infinite riches in Jesus, He giveth, and giveth, and giveth again." Such is the lesson from the fathomless sea!

15.

BLEAK BEACH

The day was dark, and the fierce winds coming in off the icy bay had whipped up the sea into a cauldron of angry white-tipped waves. Along the desolate beach struggling against the elements trying to halt my forward progress and purpose, I strolled, a solitary figure against the backdrop of a raging ocean, a tempestuous sea. Behind me high sea-cliffs separated me from the coastal village of Eastport. I was alone, but really not alone in this bleak-winter's walk.

I often went to Greenlaw Beach to think and meditate during my five year pastorate at the Washington Street Baptist Church. It became a haven for me against the newness of my first city pastorate. (Eastport was officially a city, but over the years the population declined rendering it less than a town.) I had deserted the country church for a truly downtown congregation, but it was there I discovered as David did: "The voice of the Lord is upon the waters: the God of glory thundereth . . ." (Psalm 29:30) It was on the shoreline of Passamaquoddy Bay I heard the sermonette of "The Lord on high is mightier than the voice of many waters, ye, than the mighty waves of the sea." (Psalm 93:4)

While others were warm in their hamlet lodgings, I walked alone along the stone-covered beach below the bluff. I was there to witness the power of a Maine coast winter storm. It was on that beach that I learned that storms, both external and internal, have similar characteristics. It was not the first time I travelled across the bleak beach at low tide, nor would it be the last. It became a favorite place during my stay on Moose Island. I would return for youth group campfires, family picnics, and church baptisms. But my favorite times along the shore were the "alone" times when it was me and the sea and another chance to realize: "What is man, that Thou art mindful of Him? And the son of man, that Thou visiteth him?" (Psalm 8:4), my visitations of God by the shore.

For years the turmoil in my soul had been steadily raging. I think that is why I found such a refuge in the raw power of the sea, the wind, and the tide because it was there I settled once and for all that I was His and His alone. The opinion of two difficult and depressing pastorates was that I wasn't doing my job right. Alone on Greenlaw Beach, I rediscovered that God and God alone was my Master, my Boss, and no man could come close to the power and authority of my Lord. I saw in the turbulence of the wind and the terrible waves that He alone controls the handle of power, the purpose and providence of a storm, and the start and finish of a raging sea. Though raised in the hills and hollows of a river basin in northern Maine, it wasn't until I moved to the shoals and surf of coastal Maine that I found solace of soul needed to continue on in my chosen and called profession, small town pastorates (46 years now).

I resisted the oceans draw at first because how could I leave the county of my birth, my people (farmers), and the place I thought God wanted me to minister? I had been away from Aroostook for nine years, and I had only returned for a short seven years. Now God was calling me away to a world as foreign as India. But the wise, Almighty God in His perfect providence knew I needed Eastport and its bleak beaches more than Eastport needed me. When doubts would arise about service and sermons, I would leave my in town office for my office on the shore. Alone with my Boss, listening to His powerful voice in the midst of a storm, a voice that could blocked out all others, I could and would always find my purpose and God's plan on that strip of sandy, rocky beach. Whenever things get tough for me, I return to the nearest bleak beach and hear again "the voice of God."

16.

CHANGING COASTLINES

I have never kept track of how many days I have spent on the coastlines of the world, but my recent seven days on the coast of New Jersey and the barrier island they call Long Beach proved again in my mind that no two days on the shore are ever exactly the same. Whatever bit of beach you are walking today will, if you return to it tomorrow, be changed or altered; or, if you walked along a shoreline yesterday, the same coastline you stroll today will have changed overnight. I think in part this is the great appeal of the seashore, the shoreline, the coastline—that ever changing appearance that is constantly being changed by the rolling waves, the rising tides, and the rumbling surf.

If it isn't the water that changes the topography of the shore, the change of angles of the sun will create shadows on the sand that alters the contours of the shifting sands. Some mornings the shoreline seems rugged against the soft light of the dawn; whereas at night with the setting sun the beach glows golden in the surf. During other days that same beach shore is gray against a gathering storm, and then there is that covering fog that sends a mist over the shoreline creating a damp, soaking, sand land. The sea spray off the ocean can change the shore. Add to that the rushing surf and the wind and waves, and you must notice that the water off shore is always eroding, craving, and changing the coastline. It might be a summer hurricane, a winter gale, a spring storm, or an autumn rain that changes things along the shoreline. Then there are the tides, the ebb, and the rising tides shaping the coastline with the unrelenting gravity of the moon, the immeasurable power of the ocean, and the titanic influence of the wind moving, making, and manicuring the beach into a new creation each and every day you spend on your bit of beach.

Jesus, the divine Creator of the coastlines, walked, as we do now, on similar shorelines. Luke 6:17 speaks of ". . . the sea coast of Tyre and Sidon . . ." (Where my daughter and I walked in May of 2010!) For me, it was on the seacoast of Melbourne, the seacoast of California, the seacoast of Maine, and the seacoast of Kerala that I watched the awesome movement of the tides on the coastline. With amazing precision the ocean filters and moves billions of tons of water from the depths to the shallows molding the shoreline sand into wonderful patterns. Like our mighty God who never slumbers nor sleeps (Psalm 121:4), the ocean neither slumbers nor sleeps. Hour after hour, day after day, month after month, and year after year the tide changes, the water changes, the wind changes and in the changing the coastline changes. The sand is sharpened and sculptured into a myriad of schemes and with each new walk along the sea edge we get to see once again the hand of the divine Designer at work. The ocean is never finished, the impact of the tide never done. There seems to be that constant and continual attempt to make perfect perfection.

For me, the most dramatic change on the coastline takes place either at high tide or low tide. At high tide the beach is at its smallest, but at low tide the beach can expand to unbelievable limits. Where the trillions of tons of water come from to fill in every cove and inlet and bay and shoreline amazes me. With each action of the surging of the incoming tide and the draining of the outgoing tide the seascape is transformed. The mantle of the sea covering the land and then the mantle of the land seemingly pushing the sea backwards, deposits a new image on the face of the shore. For me, the changing of the coastline is a metaphor of life itself. Surely you have noticed that no two days of your life have been the same. I learned long ago, long before my first walk on a beach that the One that changes the coastline is the same One that changes the days of my life.

17.

EILAT EXPERIENCE

We arrived in the paradise of Eilat just in time for supper, but early enough so we had time afterward to walk down through this coastal town. In 1947 Israel was given this seven-mile long coastline, and it rapidly developed into a trading port and tourist resort. We also arrived in time to watch the sun set over the Red Sea from our third story room in the Adi Hotel. We had a wonderful view of the Gulf of Eilat, the cliffs of Edom (yes, they looked red in the sun), and Jordan today on the far shore (just 4 miles away). After a traditional Israeli dinner, Marnie and I left our companions to walk the two blocks to the Red Sea. I had known the story of the children of Israel walking through the Red Sea (Exodus 14:29) all of my life, and I was determined to at least walk in its waters. Little did I know what the morning would bring, but for that moment an evening walk to its shore would wash the dust of the wilderness of Paran off my feet.

Since my return from Israel a lot of people have asked the question, "What was it like?" For those that have asked me about Eilat, I have replied, "It was a lot like walking down through Bar Harbor!" I live about twenty miles from this world-famous, tourist town on the coast of Maine. Located next door to one of the most popular national parks in America, Acadia National Park, Bar Harbor is what we in Maine call a "tourist trap." Its only reason for existing is to draw visitors from around the world to witness the seascape that is Maine made up of rocky shores, boiled lobster, and downeast hospitality. Just a few days ago we were asked by some friends of ours to dine with them at the Jordan Pond House, a very popular eating place in Acadia Park. When we arrived, the parking lots were full, and we didn't see a Maine license plate on any of the cars until we left. Even the car we were in was from Pennsylvania. Unless you are a resident, most locals spend very little time on Mount Desert Island in the summertime because of all the tourists, but the rest of the year the place and its beauty is all ours. Eilat was exactly like that. As Marnie and I tried to find the water, we had to wade through hundreds upon hundreds of vacationers. Eilat is the Atlantic City of Israel, and we soon discovered our paradise in the wilderness had a dark side.

We had left traditional Israel in Jerusalem and Beersheba. (Remember, this was the Jewish holyday of Pentecost. From what I saw in Eilat, Pentecost, whether Jewish or Christian, was not being celebrated.) Eilat was secular Israel in every way I wished it wouldn't be. Our Eden had discovered and tasted of "the tree of the knowledge of good and evil," but unlike Adam and Eve there seemed to be no shame. The women and men walked around nearly naked. The boardwalk had its fine shops, but also the bad shops. Eilat was a party town, and the lifestyle of the rich and famous could be seen everywhere. Marnie and I walked by the neon and the naked in search of the sea (Both Marnie and I love the sea, whether the Gulf of Maine, the Pacific Coast, or Indian Ocean off Kerala, and wherever we have traveled we have best loved our times by the sea and now for Marnie it is the coastline of California where she lives with her husband and two children.), and, sure enough, after about a ten-minute walk we could hear it lapping on the beach, even over the noise of the revelers and rioters. It was pitch dark by the time we found the shore, and few were on the sandy beach enjoying the cooler night air and the refreshing water. Most had been drawn to the city lights as the prodigal in Jesus' famous parable (Luke 15:13), but for Marnie and me it was the water that called us. I took off my shoes and waded knee deep into its famous stream and for a few brief moments heard nothing but the rolling surf and felt the soft sand engulf my weary feet. The lesson in this is clear: *when the world tries to engulf, you find a shoreline and walk in its surf until the noise of the world disappears.*

18.

SURF SNORKELING

The Red Sea lies between Egypt and Arabia and has two very distinct arms. The western body of water is called the Gulf of Suez where the famous "canal" is located and where the children of Israel crossed from Egypt to Sinai, or so the tradition says. This section of the Red Sea is 190 miles long. The eastern branch is called the Gulf of Aqaba (Arab name) or the Gulf of Eilat (Jewish name). This section of the Red Sea is 112 miles long, and I have come to believe that it was here, about 50 miles south of Eilat, that the children of Israel actually crossed the Red Sea at a place called Pihahiroth (Exodus 14:1, 9) from Sinai into the land of Madian (Acts 7:29). Today, Israel has a naval base there, and it is a major seaport as well. While we were there we watched a huge car-carrying ship sail into port, and our tenth day in Israel began near the spot where those cars were being off loaded. What we did that morning quickly jumped into one of the top five things I experienced in the entire trip to Israel: snorkeling in the Red Sea.

We left the Adi Hotel for the Coral Reef Beach National Park around eight. Now I knew why we had stopped at the IBEX Campus. We had picked up scuba gear for our morning of snorkeling. We left the commercial section of Eilat for a rural stretch of beach about three miles up the western shore. We stopped just short of the Israeli checkpoint that would take us into Egypt. From the sandy beach we could see back into Eilat with all the high rise hotels along its narrow shore. We could see Aqaba across the gulf with the red cliffs behind it. The water off shore was a sky blue, but the water near shore was a greenish blue. We would soon find out why. Neither Marnie nor I had snorkeled before, but there was in our midst a man who had been raised in the Bermuda. Ron Shearer and his wife Daphne were on the trip as a graduation present for Ron who had just finishing Dallas Theological Seminary, and he had snorkeled all his life. After a few quick instructions, I was off on my first snorkeling adventure over the reefs of the Red Sea.

You must understand that I am not a water lover or a swimming fan, never have been. At first I thought I wouldn't do it, but eventually decided that I was here and this was the Red Sea, so why not. I am so glad I didn't back out. For the first time I witnessed God's beauty in the sea. As I rode on the back of the Red Sea, the wind (it was a windy day so they only let us swim with the tide) carried me from the northern pier of the reserve to the southern pier. The colors were brilliant and the fish were friendly. The bottom of the sea floor was covered with multicolored coral. The water was so clear nothing escaped my eye. I saw small colorful fish everywhere, and they were not afraid to check me out, swimming right up to my facemask. The colors of the fish and coral were a rainbow with deep reds, violet purples, many shades of orange, and blues beyond imagine! The noise of the world was lost and the peaceful solitude was divine. I will say it was the most relaxing and quiet hour of the trip. As I parted the water of the Red Sea with my swimming strokes, a new world opened up to me. As I dove under the surface, a new reality of God's aquatic creation filled my senses. Marnie followed in my wake enjoying every wave as well. I now understood what the Psalmist was praising God for when he wrote: "When I consider . . . the work of Thy fingers . . . the fish of the sea, and whatsoever passeth through the paths of the sea. O Lord our God, how excellent is Thy name in all the earth!" (Psalms 8:3, 8, 9) I can now say that I have taken a trip through one of the paths of the sea, and what an amazing trip it was. And to think the Almighty parted this same sea for His children to walk across on dry land. (Exodus 14:21-22)

19.

TIDE THANKSGIVING

When you live on an island off the Gulf of Maine, the ocean seems to be everywhere. Its flow engulfs the rocks along the shore, fills the inlets, and deposits the debris from a hundred storms on the shoreline. On the bright days the ocean is bright and shining, but on those dark days of stormy clouds and boisterous winds it is gray and dull. No matter the mood of the ocean, the tide will proclaim its praise in a patterned and precise way. I love the way the Psalmist put it: "Let the heaven and the earth praise Him, the seas, and everything that moveth therein." (Psalm 69:34) One of the steady and consistent moving parts of the sea is the thankful tide.

Day by day the tide pulses back and forth like a gigantic wave. It is not a noisy clamor of praise like the roar of the surf, but a still and silent praise that only God can hear and only man can see. I have watched for hours the changing of the water levels on various beaches of the world. One of my family's favorite is the shoreline around Thompson Island, a small island that is located between the mainland of Maine and Mount Desert Island. Many years ago man built a causeway connecting Thompson Island, the Maine coast, and the more famous island of Mount Desert where Acadia National Park and Bar Harbor are located. Thompson Island is very small, maybe twenty acres, and just a going-through place to get to the more attractive attractions in Acadia, but somebody thought it would be nice to create a picnic area on the inland shore, and it is there I have taken family and friends for cookouts and to watch the incoming and outgoing tides.

Over my twenty-five plus years of visiting this tranquil and therapeutic place, I have watched the tide move driftwoods from spot to spot, shift stones on the shore, and rearrange the contour of the narrow beaches. I have often meditated on these changes and have seen in the work of the tide the eternal thanksgiving to its Creator.

Are we as thankful for the "tide" that sweeps in and through our lives? When we accepted the Lord Jesus Christ as our Saviour, we were flooded like an incoming tide with the Holy Spirit (I Corinthians 12:13). This was certainly the "high tide" that began our relationship. As I write this sermonette I am just a few days away from my 59th spiritual birthday. I remember clearly that Sunday morning when I felt for the first time the Holy Spirit sweeping into every secret cove and private inlet of my life, filling every crack and crevice with His presence. But over the years, I have also felt because of my own neglect and negligence that I was at a "low tide" in my relationship with my Lord. I had sinned, or I had drifted away. I felt empty like the cove behind Thompson Island, just a rocky, muddy bay. But just when it seemed it was permanent, I felt that forgiving surge start to return. I watch, as I do on Thompson Island, that patient, relentless push of God's Spirit tide coming back. Only the fulness of the Almighty has the ability to fill again, to once again gain a "high tide" in my life. I know the tide is thankful when it once again surrounds Thompson Island, and I ought to be filled with praise when God fills me (Ephesians 5:18). The shoreline doesn't cover itself. It is covered by the ocean, and so with us and God. The seashore doesn't change itself. It is changed by the tide, and so are we by God. The sea edge doesn't grow in size by itself. It is shaped by the ocean, and so are we in God. The alterations and rearrangement of the shoreline is the natural work of the tides, just like the changes and contours of our life is the eternal work of the Spirit of God (Genesis 1:2 "And the Spirit of God moved upon the face of the waters."), and for this we ought to be grateful, thankful, and full of praise just like the ocean tide.

20.

SOAKING STORM

All my years living in northern Maine, winter was for snow storms. Rarely did it rain from December to March in Aroostook County. You can imagine my surprise when I moved to the downeast coast of Maine. The warmer ocean waters more often than not brought winter rain, not winter snow. Washington County in the winter taught me a wonderful lesson about location, location, location in the providence of God.

Sometimes a winter on the coast of Maine can be nearly snowless. Despite the occasional Arctic blast, most wet storms come up from the south and often with them warmer air. If the cold isn't established, the moisture will fall as cold rain versus wet snow. In northern Maine, two hundred and fifty miles from the coast, the cold comes early and only deepens as the winter progresses, but on an island in the Gulf of Maine the warmer waters often insulate the island from the colder mainland air. That warmer air results in the liquid stuff versus the white stuff. Granted, sometimes it falls as freezing rain which for me is worse than snow, but on Moose Island the air temperature often stayed just above freezing, and rain was the result. A few years ago I watched one of these wintry storms come up the coast, and I learned a wonderful precept.

By morning thick, dark banks of clouds began to move into Passamaquoddy Bay. They were being pushed rapidly toward the shoreline by strong southerly winds. Combined with southern moisture and sea vapor, the clouds became gray and great with rain. The warmer stormy winds had pushed the cold air north of Bangor, and while my home county of Aroostook was in the path of a classic "nor'easter," we only got a winter rain. As the darkness descended on my afternoon, I stood before the big picture windows of the Washington Street Baptist Church sanctuary and watched the gathering storm and the first drops of rain. It was only a matter of time before the rain fell in torrents, more spring or summer rain. I was a bit sad I must admit because I love to watch a heavy snowfall in January, but it was then I learned something that I have never forgotten.

    I had been working on an upcoming lesson on the life of Elijah for my prayer meeting challenge. For three and a half years the nation of Israel had been locked in a terrible drought. The land was parched, and the people were thirsty. Only after Elijah's contest with the prophets of Baal on Mount Carmel was done would the rain return, but where did it come from? Like the storm I was watching on an island off the coast of Maine, it came from the sea. "And said unto his servant, Go up now, look toward the sea. And he went up and looked, and said, there is nothing. And he [Elijah] said, go again seven times. And it came to pass at the seventh time, that he said, Behold, there ariseth a little cloud out of the sea, like a man's hand . . . and it came to pass in the meanwhile, that the heaven was black with clouds and wind, and there was a great rain . . ." (I Kings 18:43-45) It was then and there that I understood this famous Biblical story and its meaning. This lesson came back to me again in 2010 when from the top of Mount Carmel I had a chance to see the Mediterranean Sea from a clearing in the trees. From the bluff I saw just how close Elijah's servant was to the sea that revealed that first storm cloud. The lesson: only an ocean storm can produce enough water to quench a thirsty land. Only a storm from the sea could create enough moisture to relieve a three and a half year drought. Recently in California a record drought was wiped out because of a series of massive storms from the Pacific Ocean. In Elijah's weather miracle, he called it ". . . a sound of abundance of rain." (I Kings 18:41) I now have heard that sea sound and know it is the voice of God.

21.

DIVINE DESIGN

I strolled barefoot along the wave-washed sands of Casperson Beach in Venice, Florida. My wife and the Clarks (Danny and Lori) were searching for shark's teeth on the shore as I pondered this grand design God called "seas" (Genesis 1:10). As I walked in and out of the rolling surf, my mind floated to such verses as "Thou, even Thou, art Lord alone; Thou hast made heaven, the heaven of heavens, with all their host, the earth, and all things that are therein, the seas, and all that is therein, and Thou preservest them all; and the host of heaven worshippeth Thee!" (Nehemiah 9:6) I came to the conclusion that this strand of sand I was strolling over was not there by accident, and it was exactly where the Master designer wanted it. Despite the magnitude of this beach, which was the longest and biggest I had seen up to that time (I would see grander beaches in the future in California.), it was a world in itself made up of smaller parts for small pleasures for people like me. I stooped over to grab a handful of warm sand. It not only felt nice on my winter-weary feet, but its warmth was soothing to my tired hands. My church family had sent my wife and me to the gulf side of Florida to rest and recover from many years of constant service to an ever-growing membership. Never having been to Florida, I wondered how I could rest in a retirement community of well over 500 units. I questioned the ability to relax and get refreshed when I would be spending eight days with six couples from that same church. (Emmanuel at the time had a group of "snowbirds" that spent the winter months of Maine in sunny Florida.) Yet as the grains of Casperson Beach sand ran through my fingers and surrounded my toes, I learned one of the purposes for God's divine design of the seas, the sands, and the surf.

As the foaming breakers splashed gently across my path, I thought my Creator had made this all for me. Surely on that day in the middle of January there were hundreds of others enjoying that same beach, but they quickly disappeared as I like ". . . the hosts of heaven . . ." above began to worship and praise the Almighty. With each oscillation of the waves, I was lost in "the wonder of it all." I recognized that amid the gigantic gulf spread out before me was an Eternal Presence. I looked far up the shoreline to see the sculpted sand dunes and how the land mass had been shifted and sized by its powerful neighbor, the seas. Danny told me that almost the entire western coastline was just like Casperson Beach, hundreds of miles created by the uncompromising seas and thousands of years of shaping and sanding, and for what? On that day I realized that the "what" was me! God in His wise providence knew that in a future day one of His servants would need the calming, clearing therapy of a sandy shore caressed by a soft surf.

I walked to a solitary spot well up the beach where a few were looking for shark's teeth, basking in the sun, or walking in the surf. The morning sky was bright blue with no clouds in sight, but I was a bit blue. The stress and strain of a big ministry was getting to me, but as the wavelets washed over my feet and as the warm sun bathed my back like a pair of hands massaging my weary body, I began to feel that soothing touch of God. My mind wrapped in a wonderful peace burst forth in gratitude and gratefulness for the privilege and honor of being on one of God's masterfully designed beaches. My heavenly Father knew my physical needs so well that He designed this combination of sea, surf, and sand to rest a tired soul in the middle of life's winters. As I neared fifty (I am 66 at the compiling of this sermonette), the unmistakable evidence has become very clear to me that I was also a part of God's divine design, and He would care for me.

22.

WEATHERING WINDS

After living five years on an island off the coast of Maine, I have come to a healthy respect for the power of the sea and the winds that came off the ocean in Passamaquoddy Bay. I use to stand on a sea cliff on Shackerford's Head on Moose Island and watch for hours the rising and the falling of the tides from the Gulf of Maine and feel the powerful breezes off the cool waters. The tides were a force to be reckoned with on their own, but when the wind began to blow and a gale began to develop off shore, it was then I realized that even the ocean had its match.

Shackerford's Head was one of my sanctuaries in my final years as pastor of the Washington Street Baptist Church in Eastport, Maine. I only wished I had found that sacred spot years before. It took a good ten-minute walk through a small swamp and scrub trees to reach its lofty knoll overlooking the bay, but once there you were instantly alone with your Maker. Few people took advantage of its unique attributes so more often than not I had the view and the vista to myself. It was there on that rocky height I learned that even the sea obeys the winds, and that the miracle of the Red Sea crossing by the children of Israel (Exodus 14:21: "And Moses stretched out his hand over the sea; and the Lord caused the sea to go back by a strong east wind all that night, and made the sea dry land, and the waters were divided.") was in fact a divine precept that I have come to call "the weathering wind."

Shackerford's Head was a place the song writer wrote about when he penned "... and on a clear day you can see forever!" From Shackerford's Head you could see through your spiritual eyes straight into the portals of Heaven. I don't know why, but it is true that in such places I feel much closer to God even though I know and believe that God is always near no matter where you are. Abraham must have had a Shackerford's Head in his life when he saw a city "... whose builder and maker is God" (Hebrews 11:10). I could see in my mind's eye the same thing when on a clear day, late in the afternoon, the ocean winds would begin to pick up. At first it was just a slight breeze against your face which I ignored at first because the power of the site drew your sight and the winds were unable to change your focus. The Canadian island of Campobello off the American town of Lubec was highlighted by the International Bridge that linked the two land masses as the sun reflected brightly off the steel structure. It was then I began to notice the breeze picking up and the force of the wind fluttered my clothes and blowing my hat off my head. Within a short time a mighty gale was nearly blowing me off my observation platform. As the winds picked up speed, I recalled the story of the Red Sea crossing that I had heard since a kid. It was then the "east wind" became a reality for the first time. I had always believed it, but now I was experiencing it. I watched the bay of water struggle against the increasing gale. I noticed the fight for control of direction. The water of Passamaquoddy Bay soon lost control because the breeze soon had the sea in its windy grip.

I have often since that day, like I am on this day as I write this sermonette from the seashore, pondered the spiritual application of my Shackerford's Head experience. Jesus told Nicodemus (John 3:8) that His Holy Spirit would be like the wind. You can't see it, but you can certainly see what it does and feel what it is. How often have our lives been moved, changed, and controlled by that Spirit wind just like the day the winds off the ocean took over the waters of the bay off Moose Island. How often have we fought to do our own thing and go our own way when the "weathering winds" took over.

23.

COCKY COCKLESHELL

At the very start of this sermonette I want my reader to know that I am no expert on seashells. Actually, I know literally nothing about them other than the ability to pick them off a beach. I will honestly tell you that it wasn't until I took a trip to Florida that I even spent much time pondering or meditating on the significance of seashells. Before that trip I don't believe I had spent one minute even hunting for seashells. Let us just say that seashells were not a priority in my life seeing I lived 250 miles from the nearest shoreline or coastline. However, on a wonderful spring day in winter I walked hand in hand with my dear wife along Nokomis Beach for the sole purpose of looking for seashells. As I write this devotional, I have a niece that has started an internet company with the singular purpose of selling her handmade crafts made of seashells she has picked up on the beaches along the Jersey Shore. So is there a spiritual lesson we can learn from seashells?

I also want to be very clear that as Coleen and I slowly walked the sandy shore in search of seashells, I was not thinking about seashells, but rather spiritual things. I was on vacation, and it was our last day in the warmth of a Florida winter that was better than a Maine summer day. However, as we stooped and stopped to examine the thousands of shells scattered along the shore, the experience was being recorded in this minister's memory. As it often does that memory eventually wanders to spiritualization of a seemingly insignificant event. So on the day we in Maine are facing our fourteenth snow storm of the season (yes, I count them, but unlike the weather people I haven't started to name them yet) I sit before my computer screen thinking of the simple warmth of that Monday afternoon on Nokomis Beach with my wife and a spiritual principle I can highlight and underline through a "cockleshell."

The context of this lesson comes from these words from Job: "The measure thereof is longer than the earth, and broader than the sea." (Job 11:9) The context of this verse is this thought-provoking question: *"Canst thou by searching find out God?"* (Job 11:7) The dictionary tells me that another name for a cockleshell is "a scallop shell." Were there any scallop shells on Nokomis Beach that day? Remember I know nothing about seashells. I can't tell you the difference from one shell to the other. The only way my wife and I knew what to look for is that we bought a postcard that had on the front the most abundant seashells on that beach with their names. It amazed me after looking in the shops and witnessing the scores of people on the beach just how many people spend their time searching for seashells and missing the sovereignty of God. I saw so many cocky cockleshells lying smugly on the sands of Nokomis Beach that day. Just like their counterparts in the surf these human cockleshells think they have found all they need in "a thimbleful of seawater." They wander the beach shore of Florida looking for cockleshells instead of the Creator. The Almighty is there but they look beyond Him trying to find a treasure in the surf instead of asking the "Treasure" (read the story that Jesus told in Mathew 13:45-46) into their hearts.

The measure of the Almighty is ". . . broader than the sea," so how do people miss Him? We are all like a shell in the sand along the surf in comparison to God, yet we can't see Him. A little life for a little time lost in the wilderness and vastness of an ocean of eternity, and we search not for Him, but He seeks us (Luke 19:10). The Psalmist writes: "When I consider Thy heavens, the works of Thy fingers, the moon and the stars, which Thou hast ordained; what is man, that Thou art mindful of him? And the son of man, that Thou visitest him?" (Psalm 8:3, 4) As I travelled two thousand miles to search for an insignificant cockleshell, Christ travelled from Heaven in search of a "cocky cockleshell" like me!

24.

MARRIAGE MESSAGE

I just have to record this sermonette because of the uniqueness of the situation and the two special young people that created this family memory on Memorial Day weekend.

Marriage proposals are as different as the couples involved. Some propose at a baseball game, write the question in the sky, or a myriad of other ways. Over my 44 years in the pastorate I have been involved in nearly one hundred weddings, either directly or indirectly. One of the first questions asked when a couple gets engaged is "How did he propose?" Just a few months ago my wife and I were in a bit of a disagreement over how I asked her to marry me. I will admit I had lost track of a few of the details (it was in 1972), and the old brain is beginning to fail me a bit now. For many months Coleen wouldn't give me a hint to reengage the old memory, but eventually she did, and it all came back. (My proposal was in the form of three questions, not one.) When I heard how Brandon asked my niece Alyssa to marry him, I knew I had never heard of that one before. To make it more special he did it on a sea shore in a place I had just visited a couple of months before, so I could see the proposal in my mind's eye as if I were there to witness it.

The beaches along the coastline of Long Beach Island are romantic enough without the addition of young love. Brandon and Alyssa had been raised together by "best-friend" couples. They attended school together, went to the same church together, and became best friends in childhood.

However, as they neared adulthood their feelings for each other changed into love and over the last few years it has grown into marital love. Marriage was inevitable, but a decision to finish college first postponed the date far into the future. That is until Brandon graduated last spring, but Alyssa sought a Master's in Music from Yale University. Unknown to the family, plans were being made following Alyssa's graduation in the spring of 2018, but when to ask the question, and where to ask the question, and how to ask the question?

For years the young lovers had visited the Jersey Shore together with Alyssa's parents. They had fallen in love with the sea and what came from the sea. Alyssa to this day makes homemade crafts out of Atlantic Ocean seashells and sells them on her own website through the internet. Brandon must have thought what a wonderful place to propose, and when he discovered that his family and Alyssa's family were spending the Memorial Day weekend of 2017 together at Alyssa's parent's cottage, the when and where were set, but the how remained. Numerous times Brandon had watched the ocean breakers crash on shore depositing a variety of things on the sandy breach. Ezekiel described it ". . . as the sea causeth his waves to come up" (Ezekiel 26:3). And then he thought of the old tradition of "a message in a bottle." It wasn't hard for him to get away while the families arrived and plant a bottle with the message "Will You Marry Me" in it along a sandy strip just up the shore from the cottage. And it wasn't hard or unusual to ask Alyssa to go for a walk up that same beachfront.

Why I feel honored to tell this story is the fact that night after the proposal, after Alyssa found her message in a bottle along a favorite strip of surf on Long Beach Island, Brandon and Alyssa called Uncle Barry and Aunt Cookie (what all our nephews and nieces call Coleen) to tell them of their up and coming wedding (summer of 2018). As we talked with the excited couple, I could hear in my inner ear the thundering waves and see in my memory eye the edge of the ocean, the blue of the sky, and the boiling waves lapping against a bottle stuck in the sand, and the wonderful joy found in that bottle.

25.

WEATHER'S WORKSHOP

Over the last year and a half I have been teaching the book of Job. Most people know of Job's three friends (Job 2:11), but perhaps Job's best friend was the fourth man to speak to him, Elihu. In Elihu's lengthy discourse he said: "Fair weather cometh down of the north . . ." (Job 37:22) Being from northern Maine originally, I believe in this bit of meteorological truth. ("Which made the heaven, and earth, the sea, and all therein is: which keepeth truth forever" Psalm 146:6.) In Maine, more often than not, good weather comes from the north. If foul weather invades our State, more often than not, the south is always to blame. For the last 31 years I have lived on the downeast coast of Maine. In that time I have come to the understanding that God's weather workshop for Maine weather is located in the Gulf of Maine. Without a doubt the Atlantic Ocean affects our weather on the Coast of Maine more than any other ingredient.

It is in the restless seas that most weather systems are formed. Despite the fact that storm fronts are created thousands of miles out in the oceans, it is only when they slam into the mountains along the shore or the land masses in their way that they release their much needed moisture. Year after year and century after century, we owe our productivity to the waters that come from the sea because in that filtered and purified water comes the life-giving liquid that is cycled through the weather. I believe the Almighty created the vast seas to bless the tiny bit of ground we call home.

What amazes me most about this wonderful workshop is man's fascination with it. We have weather satellites watching that weather workshop. We have weather radar that can judge direction, amount, and kind. We have weather reporters that constantly and continually update us on the current weather condition. We have weather channels that broadcast 24/7 the temperature, the forecast, and any warnings of severe weather heading our way. I read somewhere that the weather channel is now one of the most watched channels on television. While in Florida a few years back during a mid-winter break, we were told by our guests that we needed to keep an eye on the weather channel. It seems that a dangerous weather front was forming in the Gulf of Mexico. Over the next few days we listened with interest for the gathering storm. Eventually the ocean storm arrived overnight, a night we were staying in Nokomis, Florida. I must admit I slept through my only Florida storm. The next morning the grass was wet, there were a few more pinecones on the ground than normal, and the flag on the front porch was blown down, but that was it. No big deal, just another ocean storm beating itself to death.

As I thought about that southern storm, I was reminded how little has changed since the days of Jesus. "The Pharisees also with the Sadducees came, and tempting desired Him that He would shew them a sign from heaven. He answered and said unto them, when it is evening, ye say, it will be fair weather: for the sky is red. And in the morning, it will be foul weather today: for the sky is red and lowering. O ye hypocrites, ye can discern the face of the sky, but cannot discern the signs of the times?" (Matthew 16:1-3) Why did the mighty Creator give us this wonderful weather workshop to observe and study? Was it just so we would be warned when a severe southern storm was approaching our coast? Did God give us the ability and the wherefore to discern the sky and the sea so we would get our snow shovels out in preparation for a seashore snow or our umbrellas for a seacoast shower? No! God created the weather systems and the weather workshop we call the oceans that we might come to know and understand Him better.

26.

BEACH BORDERS

One of my most favorite pass times while living in Eastport, Maine, was to walk along the sea edge on Greenlaw Beach at ebb tide. With Passamaquoddy Bay at its lowest, Moose Island nearly doubled in land size and groundmass. With the receding water and the shrinking ocean come sights and sites only seen on the ebb tide. Designs in the sea floor unequalled by the master craftsmen of mankind are revealed and exposed for one's viewing. Small sea creatures unseen during high tide are now visible for inspection and observation. It seems as if the sea itself is tame and timid at ebb tide. It is smaller and not so threatening, or so it appears to a land lover like me. It was on such walks along the shore of Greenlaw Beach that I learned that life itself has an ebb and a flow, and the good Lord of the universe has predetermined the borders for both. God told Job, "Or who shut up the sea with doors, when it brake forth . . . and said, hitherto shalt thou come, but no further: and here shall thy proud waves be stayed?" (Job 38:8, 11)

    Aren't we glad as land creatures that the sea is not in control of its borders, nor has a mind of its own? As you watch the turning of the tide along Greenlaw Beach, you wonder if the incoming tide will ever stop. I remember well the afternoon I stayed to watch the entire tide come in. It started over two hundred feet from the hill line. There were old timbers from past piers and distinct rock formations on the seafloor that were surrounded and then covered first, but within the passing afternoon all obstacles once visible were swallowed and submerged in the rising surf. Even the stone fireplace we used for youth group meetings and outings and family picnics were soon under water. Within a few hours the tide was lapping against the grass along the shore. The once dry beach was wet and covered. It seemed that the tide was about to engulf the trees and shrubs scattered along the ocean's edge, but then it happened.

Quietly and quickly, suddenly and immediately, the surging, advancing water just stopped. It was freely rolling in, and then it came to a complete stop. There were no natural barriers that stopped its progress up the beach because I had watched all such barriers and obstacles slowly surrender to the advancing water. Then as if an invisible hand reached down, the tide just stopped. The water would and could come no further. The waters of Passamaquoddy Bay had reached it predetermined border for that day. My friend's house on the bluff was safe as it had for the thousands of days it stood on that shoreline. My neighbors in Eastport were safe as they had been for hundreds of years since the town was founded. The power of the ocean just a few hours before that seemed unstoppable was now stopped. The mighty push of the waves that rolled over everything in their path that seemed invincible was not vanquished. The foam and froth that floated on the top of this uncontrollable sea was now under control. The waves and the wavelets that splashed and crashed over every foe was now checked, but by what?

The Lord told Job that He was the One that had given the sea its borders. It was the Almighty that put limitations on the oceans: *"Thou hast set a bound that they may not pass over; that they turn not again to cover the earth."* (Psalm 104:9) Before God told Job, Job understood these beach borders when he said, "He hath compassed the waters with bounds . . ." (Job 26:10) The Creator knew the power of the proud sea so He put limits, boundaries, and a line in the sand if you will, where the waters of the seas and the oceans could not pass. I have learned in life that so too does my Heavenly Father set limits on my life. I can only go so far, and He will step in and stop my advance.

27.

BEAUTIFUL BREAKERS

The Hebrews prophet Micah wrote, *"The breaker is come up before them . . ."* (Micah 2:13) I know the context of this text, so I know that he is not referring to breakers along a beach, but as the enemy laid waste the city and destroyed the citizens of that city, so too does the breakers of pounding surf try to overcome the beach and a lone beachcomber.

I have admitted already that I don't like to be on water, but I get a special thrill each time I am near water, like on a beach. What I like best of any beach are the breakers—the higher the better, the stronger the more thrilling, and the louder the best. I have discovered that winter breakers are better than summer breakers. I like big waves, not the little wavelets that come on calm days. You need an ocean storm to really create the kind of breakers I love to watch . . . from shore. It is in the surging, spilling, surfing thunder of a sea wave crashing and thrashing the shoreline that makes any trip to the coastline worthwhile. My last journey to such a shore was to Long Beach Island, New Jersey. The waves were not huge, but they were big enough to make the breakers worth watching.

There is only one other water sight and site that I am more impressed with than beautiful breakers. It is the spectacular waterfalls I have been able to visit during my lifetime. The only thing ocean-side breakers lack is height. The advantage beach breakers have over waterfalls is their sheer width. Most waterfalls are narrow in comparison to a beach that goes on for twenty-two miles (Long Beach Island). A waterfall has a roar above the volume of a beach breaker, but for me it is those few seconds as the breaker builds that makes it sound more like a song, the song of the sea that calms your heart and soothes your soul. Some waterfalls stop their roar because of lack of water as I learned in 2016 when on a visit to Yosemite National Park to see its magnificent trees and amazing waterfalls. I found the trees, but the waterfalls were dry because of the drought in California. Sometimes a walk on a beach yields a few breakers from a silent sea. Falls without water and seas without wind are not worth visiting.

Breakers are for restoration of the beach, cleansing of the shoreline, and bathing the sand in shells. My favorite beach walker is Phillip Keller. In his book "Sea Edge" he makes this wonderful application to breakers. "For just as the ocean is ever at work breaking itself over my bit of beach, so my Father's unfathomable love is ever in action spilling out upon my sin-stained soul. Had He chosen, as well He might, to confine His compassion to Himself; I would never have known the cleansing, caring impact of His life on mine." As I sat that day on Long Beach Island and watched the breakers crash in over the sandy shore near my brother's seaside cottage, I thought again of the wonderful grace and mercy of God that broke over my life through the difficult storm my wife and I had just gone through. It was the greatest of sickly storms we label as cancer. My 39-year old son lasted just six months with a deadly form of the disease. The breakers were loud and terrifying, but with each passing pulse of pain came that similar roar of God's voice that He was there in the midst of the storm. Seemingly the breakers of cancer would break us, but instead of being destroyed they only made us stronger and more faithful in believing that God knows best. I write this sermonette just two months after Scott's departure. I see now this experience because of the beautiful breakers that rolled onto our beach. With them came a love that thrilled my soul, a mercy that bathed my spirit, and a grace that subdued every doubt and fear. As with the breakers on a beach, the tide rolls in, but it also goes out, and with it takes all the debris from the shore and deposits it away; such was my experience when cancer came for a visit!

28.

BEACH BENEDICTION

I was raised a country boy not a city slicker, yet it has been to the city ministry I have been called by the Lord. Sometimes my calling and my makeup clash, and during those times I must leave the bedlam of the city for the benediction of the beach. During my last two pastorates of 31 years, I have had to compromise my wild woods aspirations for a stroll along the seashore. In 1986, the good Lord moved me from the great north woods in northern Maine to the seashore along the coast of Maine. I soon found that I could meditate and contemplate just as well on the shore as in the spruce. My harassed soul could and did find rest and reflection along the beaches just south of Ellsworth.

To this day I have to leave the babel of traffic and telephones for a silent sit on the seacoast. In the fall the trees along the shore show off their bright foliage as the summer birds head south for a warmer winter elsewhere. In the spring the evergreen are still green, but the rest of the forest along the coast waits their resurrection green to appear. It doesn't matter whether it's winter, spring, summer, or fall because the seasons might change, but the refreshing rest that a trip to the beach brings is the same. The cry of a seagull constantly seeking and searching for its next meal or the smell of a salty breeze calls me to the ocean's edge. Just the day before yesterday I asked my wife on a second date on the same day, a rarity for us. In the morning we went to Sylvia's for breakfast, our favorite eatery in Ellsworth, but for supper we packed a lunch and headed for Thompson Island, a small, tree covered bit of land between the mainland and the more famous Mount Desert Island where Bar Harbor and Acadia National Park are located. Thompson Island has been a favorite sea shore for most of our 26-year stay in Ellsworth. When we arrived, there were only a few others enjoying the cooler air (we were in our first heat wave of the summer). We had come for the sea breeze, to eat our sandwiches, and feed the seagulls, but we were there for a little mediation as well. One of the things that have often impressed me with the patriarch Isaac are these simple words in Genesis 24:63: "And Isaac went out to meditate in the field at eventide." Isaac didn't have a beach, just a field, but both will do when reflection and meditation are on your mind.

My wife and I had just come into a huge inheritance, a sum of money beyond anything we had experienced in our 44-year marriage. Throughout our ministry we have been paid just what we needed for the time and cared for in the bare minimum at times. We never thought we would be rich and were "... content with such things" as we had. (Hebrews 13:5) Yet the good Lord in his divine wisdom had granted us a fortune to take care of us in our old age. (That same week my wife had just been accepted for Medicare, and we both were now receiving Social Security.) Some people immediately rush off to a financial advisor, or a banker, or an accountant. Coleen and I took a ten mile ride to Thompson Island to ask the Granter of these funds what we were to do with them. We sought a place of contemplation on a rocky beach on the backside of a typical coastal Maine island. The devil has convinced most people, including many Christians, that earthly gain must include more gain, to make money with money. If God gave us the money, shouldn't we go to Him for financial advice?

So what was our beach benediction? It was this simple precept from the pen of James, "If any of you lack wisdom, let him ask of God, that giveth to all men liberally, and upbraideth not; and it shall be given him. But let him ask in faith, nothing wavering. For he that wavereth is like a wave of the sea driven with the wind and tossed." (James 1:5-6)

29.

SEASHORE SORROWS

This is not one of the best mornings along a sandy beach. The breeze is mid-April cool, and the sun has a thin haze covering it on an otherwise clear day. The seagulls are trying to cheer me up, but all I hear is their haunting cries. Nothing in God's glorious nature can spark any joy in my soul at the moment because this morning I walk alone, brokenhearted over the death of my soldier boy of just 39. He did not die on some God-forsaken battlefield in a far off and distant land, but in my arms, at home, with cancer.

The sandpipers dart to and fro, but even their silly dance can't break through this glum that has invaded my spirit. All days can't be ideal, idyllic, or idealistic with a bright smile. Despite the pleasant mood of the sea and the cheerful sounds of the creatures along Long Beach Island, I was not here for a vacation but a sabbatical. I was on the Jersey Shore to mourn my son's departure and grieve over the sudden sickness that took his physical life. When Paul wrote of ". . . perils in the sea . . ." (II Corinthians 11:26), I never thought I would have to take such a walk by the sea. My brother Mike had offered his house on the shore for my wife, our daughter and her family, and me as a retreat from the six-month ordeal, yes, tribulation, we had experienced. So two days after Scott's Good Friday funeral we left for Long Beach Island, one of the barrier islands off the New Jersey shore. What father ever imagines he will have to endure the peril of the death of his son? I had learned through the experiences of others that life is a series of storms and sunshine, tears and joys, tragedy and triumphs. We can believe that Jesus understands this because He had similar experiences. He told us that "In the world ye shall have tribulation, but be of good cheer: I have overcome the world." (John 16:33)

On this "off" morning along Long Beach shore I was having a hard time being of good cheer. Granted, I wouldn't want to live in a world where the weather was the same, the seasons were the same, or life itself was the same. I come from Maine where everything is a mixture. God is good at mingling nature's ingredients and life's menu to make our diet interesting, but the bitter herbs of a son's death reminds me of dismal and unwelcomed days. I knew that no day can be a perfect day, but I was learning that some days are just plain miserable and, yes, mean. That morning of sorrow along the seashore I was trying to cheer myself with: ". . . that all things work together for good . . ." (Romans 8:28) and ". . . this is the victory that overcometh the world, even our faith." (I John 5:4) I knew my theology, a minister for nearly 44 years, and I had faith, a believer for nearly 59 years, but on that bleak morning walk along Long Beach I was struggling in my sorrow.

As I wandered along the ocean's edge, I wondered what I could do to change my mood, to lift the burden and sorrow from my mind and once again feel "the joy of the Lord." The more I walked (nearly four miles that morning) the more my heart ached. When I reached the end of the shore and looked into the open ocean before me, it was then I realized that I had taken up the philosophy of the world in my time of sorrow. The world is all about go-getters. Keep on going, move beyond it, go-go-go. Life's sorrows can't be run down, overcome by go-getters, but by "stand-stillers." God has the exact opposite philosophy, and that morning as I stopped moving and stood still I found a peace in my sorrow when I remembered "Be still, and know that I am God . . ." (Psalm 46:10) and ". . . stand still, and see the salvation of the Lord . . ." (Exodus 14:13) The answer: wasn't in struggling over my sorrow, but standing still in my sorrow and allowing God to comfort my soul, sooth my spirit, and calm my mind in the grace of His love! Amen!

30.

SHATTERED SEAWALL

I read this in a book by Phillip Keller. *"In giant storms, the pressure of an ocean beating on solid stone can mount to more than 60,000 pounds to the square foot. That is the awesome equivalent of well over 30 tons of impact to one square foot of rock surface. The rock cannot long endure such battering and abuse. Some portion of it will break loose, to be flung against the shore and serve as a giant battering ram that is caught up in the waves, to grind and rumble against other boulders in the surf!"* After reading this explanation of the power of the sea, I understood what happened to a shattered seawall I once strolled by on a walk near the shore in Eastport, Maine.

The shoreline along the waterfront in Eastport is a graphic reminder of the awesome strength of the sea. An old seaport, Eastport has seen the attempts of many generations trying to control the waters of Passamaquoddy Bay. Elaborate seawalls, coastal barriers, and loading piers dot the coastline along Water Street (Main Street in most towns, but for an island city by the ocean's edge a more appropriate name). While I lived in Eastport, I pastored a small Baptist church just two blocks from the seashore. On nice days and not so nice days, I would walk from my study in the church building to clear my head by the breakwater. There in front of the store fronts was a gigantic collection of rocks strategically placed to protect the downtown from flooding and storm surge. On the clear, calm, "you can see forever" days the bay was quiet with very little wave activity, but when the wind was up and a large ocean storm hovering just off shore was brewing on the other side of Campobello Island, the bay became that "battering ram" that Phillip Keller wrote about. I would set on the shore and watch the pounding. Despite huge blocks of granite mixed with large cement blocks and reinforcing steel, the breakwater never faired very well against the hammering blows of the sea. Just in my time in Eastport (five years) the Army Corps of Engineers was constantly and continually repairing the seawall. The shoreline was always littered with thousands of tons of debris torn loose and broken up, scattered by the relentless pounding of a raging sea. Every effort of man to build something indestructible is impossible, and so it is with the plans of man versus the providence of God.

Again and again I went down and sat in silence on the huge boulders that protected the inner harbor of Eastport. Each time I would notice the wear and tear. Some stones were holding up better than others to the immense pressure of the pulverizing ocean. Some man-made objects were surviving better than others to the systematic pounding of the unrelenting sea. It was then I realized the truth of the Psalmist in relationship to the sea and its waves: "Thou rulest the raging of the sea; when the waves thereof arise, Thou stillest them." (Psalm 89:9) Are we not grateful that the Almighty on occasion "stillest them?" How long would the old seawall in Eastport or any port last if the pounding, raging water never stopped? They like us only last because the onslaught is only for a season or a storm. The good Lord has promised us through the pen of Peter that "Wherein ye greatly rejoice, though now for a season, if need be, ye are in heaviness through manifold temptations." (I Peter 1:6) What a sermonette from the seashore. Temptations, trials, tests are like the pounding sea, the raging, wind-swept ocean on our seawall, yet we survive like the Eastport seawall has survived because we only have to endure for a time, for a season, for a storm. Shattered, scared, and sore, but, like that old seawall on the downeast coast of Maine, still standing, and so am I after threescore and six years.

31.

BARELEGGED BOY

I discovered on a Florida trip that the sea edge is a wonderful place for reflection and re-examination. To find a secluded spot and a privacy place was difficult, but even among the many shore strollers, one could find communion with God.

The barelegged boy left his wife and their friends the Clarks (Danny and Lori) behind as he wandered up Casperson Beach. Despite the fact that he was a man nearly in his 50s, he felt like a lad in his shorts and tee-shirt, a child on his first walk along a sandy shore on a brand, new seashore. The weather brought back to the man-boy the summers of his youth, and he felt sixteen again. Nearly a half century of northern winters had taken a toll on this aging boy, but the winter sun of western Florida soon brought out a young-at-heart feeling in his limbs, in his muscles, and in his soul. It seemed to be the same in his spirit as he strolled along, carefree and free. Twenty-five years (44 now at this compiling) in the ministry of pastoring had cost his soul much and his body even more, but the beach and the bright sunshine seemed to lighten the load and share the burden as he wandered, wondered, and worshipped up the sandy shore, lost in meditation and memories.

The man with the boy's mind discovered on that walk that you don't have to be a man or a mystic to understand the energy of the environment he was passing through. Despite the fact I had left Florida five weeks ago today, as I put this memory on paper my wife just this morning had asked me this question, "You really haven't left Florida yet have you?" And in soul, spirit, and mind he hadn't. I have lingered longer than I ever thought I would on Casperson Beach because that special spell that so many had talked to me about had fallen over me. Before Florida I wasn't much of a beachcomber. I remember Danny telling me before the trip I would fall in love with the beaches of the Gulf of Mexico. I am now just coming to a full understanding of what he meant. It is more than a dream or dreaming dreams of warm days and warming nights. It is more than soft sunsets over calm, clear waters. It is more than the joy of staring out to sea and watching for dolphins. For me it was the contentment one finds in the company of the ocean, alone in your thoughts and thinking, walking side by side and hand in hand with the gulf as if you are walking side by side, hand in hand with the Almighty.

I watched as other barelegged boys, much older than me, sat on wave-battered rocks fishing as if they were kids again caring not whether they caught a fish or not, just grateful for being there. I watched elderly couples strolling hand in hand with their beloved as if they were young lovers on a honeymoon again. I watched individuals wading into the surf acting like children on their first trip to the beach. What was it about this Casperson Beach that brought the youth out of each of us, this tranquility of soul and spirit, that turned a section of a Florida beach into a paradise, a Shanghai, "a summer place?" Even the seagulls, terns, and pelicans seemed at peace with each other in this soothing seaside along a calming coastline.

It wasn't until I returned from my barelegged walk that I found the answer to my questions in these words from the pen of Phillip Keller: *"The warmth of the sun, the softness of the sea air, the drift of haze and sea mist wrap this bit of beach in folds of quietude. It is a spot to come with a good book, with a thick terry towel, and an hour or two to stretch the body and stretch the soul and 'extend one's spirit' to meet one's Maker in quiet communion."* Is that what Jesus was doing when it says, "And he went forth again by the sea side . . ." (Mark 2:13) Do you suppose He was barelegged.

32.

BEAUTIFUL BEACHES

After every seaside stroll, after every sea edge walk, and after every seashore visit, there remains in the mind a remarkable beautiful beach. Not just the inward remembrance of a wave-splashed shore sparkling in the radiance of a summer sun, but an outward reflection of a beautiful beach etched in sand and outlined by a carved cliff face. Over my sixty-six years of exploring my planet I have discovered some very beautiful beaches handcrafted by the Almighty Himself.

The character of a beach is ever changing because it never stays static. Each day the design will change because of the waves, the winds, and the waters that transform its makeup. Every high tide will alter its appearance and, for those of us who only venture near it on the rarest of occasions, the outline will be different, the canvas will be changed, and the seascapes will be reshaped, but what will not be changed is the beauty of the beach. What makes the beach so beautiful is the continual and constant hand of God working on it as a Master Painter, a Master Sculptor, and a Master Weaver. Using the wavelets of the surf as a brush, a chisel, and a loom, He fashions every day on the beach a masterpiece unlike the day before. As every snowflake is different, so is every beach, every day, fashioned by the Divine Designer! Paul in his reply to the Lycaonian who wanted to worship him and Barnabas for their miracle of healing a cripple (Acts 14:8-12) said, "... unto the Living God, which made heaven and earth, and *the sea*, and all things that are therein." (Acts 14:15) And that includes all beaches.

Whether Casperson Beach in Florida, Sandy Beach in Maine, Caesarea Beach in Israel, Long Beach in New Jersey, Eve's Beach in Kerala, Melbourne Beach in Australia, or Valdez Beach in Alaska, everywhere there is an action, a motion, and creativity on the beach, and no two beaches are the same, identical, or the same shape, length, or size. Each beach I have visited has shown itself to be a unique masterpiece from God, formed by the ebb and flow of the combination of a restless sea and a shaping wind using tiny specks of sand to fashion and form the individual beaches. With the falling and the rising of the tides, the rivulets of sea water and the collection of granules of pebbles combine to shape the surface of the shore. The contour of the tide flats, the shaping of the sand dunes, the cutting and swirling of the beach speaks again of an unseen hand, an invisible Artist that creates a scene unduplicated by anything modern man can form. I was told the last time I was on Long Beach in New Jersey that Hurricane Sandy had literally taken all the sand off the beach in its destructive landfall. The Army Corps of Engineers had replaced the sand, but left the shaping to the sea. The beautiful beach at Long Beach was the work of man and God, but God gets the credit for the beauty.

As I walk again in my mind on the beaches I have had the privilege of exploring, there is left behind by the water of the tides and the winds off the sea a patterned expression of the Almighty. So too is the continual and constant impact of the Spirit of God on the souls of His men and women. Each life is different, fashioned and sharpened by the Holy Ghost. Each day of that life makes that life different than the day before. It is that persistence of purpose shaping and making us into the "image of His Son..." (Romans 8:29) As the water and wind work on the shore, so the Spirit works on our minds, our emotions, and our wills, conforming us, transforming us, day by day, moment by moment, into someone totally different than the person we were yesterday or the day before yesterday. A believer in Christ is a beautiful person, not as the world defines beauty, but as God sees us through the person of His Son, Jesus Christ.

33.

ELEGANT EAGLE

There it was setting in a short, leafless tree beside the Lowe River, our first Valdez eagle. I have been fascinated by the bird Adam called "eagle" for most of my life. Living in a state where there is a healthy population of the majestic fowl, I have had the privilege of seeing countless eagles over the years, but none on a sea shore. Each sighting has been a thrill whether over the massive Penobscot River while Atlantic Salmon fishing or the snow covered Branch Pond while ice fishing, I have enjoyed every encounter with the eagle. After hearing Scott's stories of eagles as thick as seagulls in Valdez, I couldn't wait till we got to the Alaskan port and Valdez Bay.

Thirty-four times in God's Holy Writ the eagle is mentioned. Is it God's favorite bird? Granted, I know that the eagles named in the Bible are not the same as our famous North American Bald Eagle. According to my research there are at least 59 species of eagles worldwide, and this magnificent bird is found on every continent except Antarctica. Haliaeetus Leucocphalus is the scientific name for the bald eagle, and by some estimates there were half a million of these birds flying over America when it was named the national bird in 1782. (Surely you know by now that Benjamin Franklin wanted to name the turkey!) The very demeanor of the eagle speaks of high flying freedom, and despite the decline (only 417 pairs in 1963) of the population in the lower 48 states, the Alaskan bald eagle has always been free-wheeling and numerous in America's fiftieth state, home to over 20,000 pairs. But on the afternoon of my first Valdez's sighting, I only saw one eagle, not the multitude of eagles I expected to see. I was hoping I would witness a verse that I had read since childhood: "For wheresoever the carcasses [and there were plenty of carcasses of dead salmon on the shores of Valdez Bay and the rivers that flowed into that bay] is, there will the eagles be gathered together." (Matthew 24:28)

Created for the Alaskan environment, bald eagles have several layers of feathers including a layer of down that insulates the eagle and makes it possible for the bird to live in the harsh climate of Alaska. Fish is the eagle's primary source of food, so it is not surprising that in Valdez where fish are plentiful that the population of eagles would also be plentiful. But on the day (August 21, 2014) we pulled into Valdez, the eagles were few and far between. We only spotted a half dozen fishing along the Lowe River leading into town so my first impression with Valdez was disappointing because of our lack of spotting numbers of eagles.

Edwin Way Teale once wrote, "Above all other birds, it is the soaring eagle that gives the most abiding impression of power and purpose in the air." Solomon, the wisest man ever to live, agreed when he wrote of the four most wonderful things he had ever seen, and first on that quartet was ". . . the way of an eagle in the air . . ." (Proverbs 30:19) We would eventually see 22 eagles in our Alaska shoreline adventure, far fewer than we imagined, but enough to fill our quest to see the world's greatest bird. Besides the eagles along the Lowe River, we saw a number flying over Valdez Bay and a few soaring. God created (Job 39:27) the eagle with broad, long wings ideal for conserving energy while in flight. Its very makeup reduces air turbulence and makes gliding easier. The experts say an eagle can attain speeds of up to 30-50 mph, and that eagles are known to travel upwards of 180 miles in a day. The eagles we saw in Valdez were not travellers because everything they needed was below them in the massive pink salmon run that was happening in Valdez Bay. There we got a glimpse of one of God's greatest creation.

34.

EAGLE ENERGY

As we watched and waited for the eagles along the shoreline of Valdez's Bay, Alaska, I knew from my study that the few eagles we saw were watching us. (I have a whole series of messages and PowerPoints on God's use of the eagle in Scripture to teach us many lessons.) One of the most amazing features of the bald eagle is its eyes. A second eyelid slides across their eyes every few seconds wiping airborne dust away, and because the lid is translucent it allows the bird to see even in mid-blink. The eagle also was created with a two-fold focusing system, one for looking sideways and the other for looking forward. As a result, the eagle's eyesight is the sharpest of any other animal and eight times sharper than the human eye. I read once that an eagle flying at a thousand feet can oversee an area of three square miles and identify a prey moving at a mile. Whether flying high or perched on a tall tree, the eagle is always on the alert for its next meal. I have seen them in tall spruce trees along the shores of Big Lake in Downeast Maine waiting for a bass to come close to the surface of the lake, and I have seen them in tall fir trees along the banks of Grand Lake Stream waiting patiently for a landlock salmon to make a mistake. One of the great thrills of the out-of-doors is to watch an eagle leave its perch for an attack or a free meal. One of the joys I had while ice fishing was the late afternoon arrival of the local eagle to get the insides of the lake trout we caught. I was looking for a similar event from the eagles of Valdez Bay.

While in Alaska I learned that one of the greatest concentrations of eagles takes place along a ten-mile stretch of the Chilkat River near Haines, Alaska. This is one of the primary wintering grounds of the Alaskan bald eagle in the months of November and December. Sometimes as many as 4,000 eagles (What a sight that must be!) gather to take advantage of the late Chum Salmon run. Scott spent his first winter in Alaska running supplies from Fort Wainwright in Fairbanks to other military based scattered around southern Alaska. A number of his winter runs was to Valdez, and though he never saw the number like in Haines, he did see the gathering of eagles that Christ foretold (Luke 17:37). We were a bit early to see such a sight for ourselves. Because the salmon runs were going on everywhere in Alaska in August, the bald eagle population was spread out, but they would gather in a few months or on the day of the judgment.

Over the day we were in Valdez, I was reminded again of my favorite Biblical eagle verse each and every time I see one of these spectacular birds. "But they that wait on the Lord shall renew their strength; they shall mount up with wings as eagles; they shall run, and not be weary; they shall walk, and not faint." (Isaiah 40:31) My mind goes back to that first Valdez eagle as it sat on it perch keeping an eye on its feeding grounds, no doubt a pool in the Lowe river where the spawning salmon congregate. It looked healthy as food was plentiful, and little energy had to be expended to find a meal. Harder and harsher days were just around the corner with the coming of autumn and the dark winter thereafter, but for now it was paradise and heaven rolled up in one season. It is with this picture I would have you ponder Isaiah's verse, a verse I have had in my memorized memory since my early twenties. It was the verse my college society chose as their motto, and yes, our mascot the eagle. Isaiah wants us to see the power of an eagle taking to flight as we recognize the strength we receive when we "wait on the Lord." The Bible is clear that as our days so shall our strength be (Deuteronomy 33:25) from the Lord. Paul taught that we can do anything through the strengthening of Christ (Philippians 4:13), and as God has given the eagle its strength, so He gives us the strength of the day.

35.

SEASHORE SALMON

As we waited to get into our motel room in the village of Valdez, we explored the small, coastal town for a place to fish. The town was crowded with the summer people (the clerk at the Best Western told us the population triples in the summer months, much like the Maine coastal community of Bar Harbor), and the motels and hotels were full and the RV and trailer parks scattered around town flashed no vacancy signs. We quickly got out of town heading for the road leading to the gigantic oil terminal on the other side of the bay. The informative clerk also said that one of the most popular fishing spots was also along that road called Allison Point where seashore salmon were in abundance.

On the way to Allison Point we passed a fish hatchery and the largest flock of seagulls I have ever seen in my life. Living on the coast of Maine for the last thirty-one years, I have seen my fair share of seagulls and large flocks here and there, but at the most a few score at a time. But as we drove beside Valdez Bay, there were hundreds upon hundreds of seagulls milling around in the air over the small stream by the hatchery. The tide appeared to be going out, and large sand bars stretched along certain sections of the shoreline. On these sand bars were hundreds of seagulls just seating or feeding on dead salmon. We eventually arrived at a large parking area, and we could see from the roadside a sandy beach below a small bluff. There were a few fishermen casting into the bay so we decided to check the situation out. Coleen stayed in the car while Scott and I walked down a narrow path to the beach. It reminded me of a few places along the coast of Maine except for the "Beware of Bears" signs. Now that was new!

Interestingly, the first person we talk to was a transplant from Maine (a lady that was married in Caribou, Maine: the town I had been born in). As I looked up and down the long shoreline, I noted that the lady in front of me was the only lady I saw in a group of about two dozen fishermen. Each was casting a large spoon into the bay along a sandy shore that was about a football field in length scattered with a small boulder or two, but most of the shore was flat and sandy. The beach went down the shoreline until a large rocky outcropping jutted into the bay. Up the shore the beach stopped at a small stream that flowed into the bay from under the roadway. I struck up a conversation with the lady because she had at her feet what I was looking for, a silver salmon. She had just caught the 15-pound beauty and was actually about to leave with her prize. When she found out that we were from Maine, she stopped to give us the lowdown on Allison Point. She had moved to Alaska with her husband and enjoyed catching dinner. She told Scott and I that we had arrived at ebb tide and that the incoming tide might hold some silvers, but most of the fish in the sea were pinks. She kind of laughed at us when we said we were going to fly fish (everybody there that day was spin fishing), but she gave us a hearty "good luck" as she headed up the bank with her salmon in hand. (Genesis 9:2)

It was then I noticed just how many fish were swimming along the shore in a few feet of water. What was even more impressive were the hundreds of dead fish washing up on the shore! I had seen a few at Montana Creek, but nothing to the numbers along Allison Point Beach. I learned from another fisherman that Valdez Bay has one of the largest pink (Humpy) salmon runs in Alaska. What made this particular section so populated with pinks was the hatchery above the beach. Most of the salmon returning had been hatched in that hatchery, and they were returning to the place they had been released. I stood amazed at the volume of fish before me, and I was even more determined to fish. Once again I was impressed with the sheer size of God's creative hand in Valdez Bay.

36.

SHORELINE SMORGASBORD

To say fishing Valdez Bay for pink and silver salmon was a unique fishing experience would be an understatement. I had never fished where the fish were so thick that they were constantly hitting your legs while you stood in the water. I thought of this line by Moses, ". . . shall all the fish of the sea be gathered together . . ." (Numbers 11:22) Scott and I waded as far into the bay as he could to get away from the dead and dying salmon near shore. Once again our biggest obstacle was the lack of aggressiveness of the salmon. Most of the fish we saw were dying, and our hope was that a few long casts further out in the bay might attract migrating "silver"! We could see the boats far off shore trolling, and we surmised they were looking for silvers, not pinks. Scott was fishing a floating line, but I had put on a fast sinking line with a huge Miramichi spring salmon fly that was a favorite of mine called Copper Renus. Within minutes I had on my first Valdez Bay pink. It was sluggish in its fight, but heavy against the strong tide that was switching and the deep water I was fishing in. Over the next two hours I landed about ten salmon all about twenty-five inches long and weighed four or five pounds. Scott didn't get a strike! It was then Scott decided to take his mother back to the motel and have some supper, but I made a different choice.

I was determined to stay and fish the complete tide (six hours long) in hopes the new tide would bring a few silver salmon near shore. Leaving me with his bear repellant (the lady from Maine said they had seen a mother and two cubs over the last two days feeding on the dead salmon washing up on shore) just in case, Scott promised to be back in a couple of hours to see how I was doing. As they drove off back to Valdez, I went back to fishing along Allison Beach. As the afternoon (we started at two) slipped away, I noticed that with each passing hour there were fewer and fewer fishermen on the beach. I began to think that the lady had misled me because by the time there was just a thin strip of sand life on Allison Point Beach, I was the only fisherman still fishing that I could see. Granted, I was periodically catching fish (I would catch 54 pinks-John 21:11—far fewer than the disciples) between 2 and 9 PM, but no silvers. I did enjoy the alone time as I always have. Fishing alone is a pleasant experience if you're catching fish as I was, and the scenery was interesting. I was hoping, as I regularly looked around, to see that mother bear and her kids, but no visits from the local grizzly family happened.

When everybody had left me at the fishing hole of Allison Point, I was joined by a pair of fishers that entertained me for the rest of the afternoon. As I casted my heavy fly into the bay and slowly retrieved it, I looked around to see what else was happening in my line of sight. It was then I saw a fish jump into the air far out in the bay. I was excited at first thinking it was an incoming school of silvers. Upon closer observation I realized it wasn't jumping salmon, but salmon being thrown by a harbor seal that was playing with his supper. As I watched closer I spotted one seal and then another as they worked their way off shore fishing as they swam. Every once and awhile, I would see an airborne salmon and watched as the throwing seal caught his cast before it hit the water. I had seen the feat on television, but in Valdez Bay it was amazing. When I thought I had seen everything, I saw something else in the water just beyond me, sea otters. Again, I had seen the creatures on television, but this was my first sighting in the wild. Between landing Valdez pinks, I was entertained by two very colorful sea creatures. I will never forget the afternoon that my only fishing companions were a couple of seals playing toss with pink salmon, and a sea otter who was having just as much success fishing as I was. I believe Jesus has a special place in His heart for fishermen, human or mammal!

37.

SCATTERED SEASHELLS

One afternoon on our only visit to the beaches of western Florida Danny (Clark) went golfing and his wife Lori was sunning herself on the shore, but Coleen and I went shell hunting along Nokomis Beach. It was our last day on a January vacation, and it was the custom of the Clarks to do whatever you wanted to do before a return to the reality of a Maine winter the next day.

I am no expert on seashells, but I did come across a few interesting spiritual precepts on my stroll with my wife up Nokomis Beach in search of a few seashells to take home for souvenirs under the caption from James: "... and of things in the sea ..." (James 3:7) Besides, we had to prove we had really been in Florida to those who didn't think that we would actually go on the Sunshine State trip.

What first impressed me was how many shells there were. Scattered here and there along miles and miles of sandy shore were thousands and thousands of seashells. The single shell on a bit of beach was rare. We discovered huge collections of shells massed together in great piles everywhere. Small ones and large ones mixed together in a mighty deposit of seashells. How they reflected the human seafarers on the beach. As one walked the shoreline there were groups of sun worshippers everywhere. Rare did you see the individual isolated from the rest. There were a few, but most on Nokomis Beach that day were moving in packs or herds. I thought of Jesus classic precept of the "many" and the "few" (Matthew 7:13-14) and the destination of each group.

What impressed me next was the fact we couldn't find hardly any perfect shells. Not only were the seashells scattered all along the beach, they were shattered all over the beach as well. Mostly all we found were bits and pieces of shells that had been battered and broken by the grinding surf against the turf. Unbroken specimens of any kind of seashell were very hard to locate in the myriad of shells along the shore. Only occasionally would we find a shell that had somehow found a sheltering crevice, a safe haven along the water's edge. Half buried in the sand, protected by a rock, the special shell had withstood the pounding tide and was now for us a special remembrance of our trip to the Gulf of Mexico. It was then I recalled another classic concept of Jesus: ". . . many are called but few are chosen." (Matthew 22:14)

What impressed me lastly was the joy that came from finding a perfect shell, a keepsake treasure, a shell worth holding onto. The value becomes clear when one realizes that out of thousands only one survives the journey from sea to sand unbroken. The scarcity of perfection keeps the shell hunter alert and vigilant in his quest to discover that beautiful bonus on a walk with his wife along a sandy shore. I thought as we sought our seashell souvenir that this is exactly what Jesus meant when He said in one of his classic parables about ". . . one sinner that comes to repentance." (Luke 15:7) According to the parable of the lost sheep and the lost silver, there was great joy when each was found, but Jesus added the explanation that "likewise, I say unto you, there is joy in the presence of the angels of God over one sinner that repenteth." (Luke 15:10) There is joy and rejoicing among the seraphim's of the Sovereign One as one in a thousand is found and brought into the family of God. Now and forever he or she will be seen as a trophy of God's amazing grace, a souvenir of Christ's visit to earth, and His numberless walks along the beaches of mankind where He discovers hidden in the sand of sin a soul worth keeping and a treasure worth the trip. Amen!

38.

FASHIONING FINGERS

Coming from a land-locked community in northern Maine, it wasn't until I moved to the coast of Maine that I saw the sea in all its amazing shapes and sizes, sites and sights. I had witnessed ". . . the finger of God . . ." (Psalm 8:4) at work in the fields and forests in the river valley of Aroostook County, but sea and surf were unknown until Moose Island. I thought I knew the magnitude and might and majesty of God, but nothing compares to the hand of God as seen in the ocean surrounding an offshore island. The Psalmist said it best of God when he wrote, "He shall have dominion also from sea to sea." (Psalm 72:8)

I felt like the magicians of Egypt the first time I watched the miracle of the tides because I said like them, ". . . this is the finger of God . . ." (Exodus 8:19) I watched as the ebb tide exposed acre upon acre of mud flats, sandy shores, and countless rock formations invisible at high tide. I walked those flats and shores to find the finger of God. Granted, there were numberless examples of the works of man hidden under the high water mark such as old anchors, old wooden piers, and even a few wooden pieces of old sailing ships of long, long, long ago. Many of these parts could be seen buried in the sand, as were old rotten pieces of timber from a former pier stuck in the mud. Old bricks from one of the many smoke stacks of former fishing factories once located along the shoreline were now a part of the surf and shore. The seashore of Eastport once was lined with sardine canning factories, but now their legacy was just a few bricks and boards. There was certainly the handprint of man on the ocean floor, but the fashioning hand of God was the best.

It was when I learned that man had once seriously pondered the possibility of harnessing the tides of Passamaquoddy Bay that I realized that there are many things the hand of man can't do. Some things are only meant for "the fingers of God." God's powerful prowess is seen in those unharnessed tides and unchanged shorelines. So many people walk the shores of Moose Island daily, but never consider that man's fingers have nothing to do with the spectacular spectacle before them in the seashore and the shoreline of Passamaquoddy Bay. I also must admit that I had never considered the remarkable displays of "the fingers of God" until I walked the coastline of Maine. What does man have to do with a flight of Canadian geese over the bay from north to south and from south to north as these majestic flocks fly year after year over these waters, flying straight on course hour after hour without the aid of compass or GPS? They like the tides are guided by the hand of God. What of the mighty whales that work their way into Passamaquoddy Bay each summer? Without electronic gadgetry or manmade navigational gear, they appear and disappear by the unseen fingers of God. Still to this day one of the greatest sights I have seen in the sea was a whale longer than the boat I was in surfacing beside us and saying hello off the Eastport side of Campobello Island. And what of the schools of fish, the livelihood of Eastport for a century and more, and their migration "... through the paths of the seas ... " (Psalm 8:8) leading them to that sheltered bay. Only "the fingers of God" could create such currents and courses for these fish.

In this mad world's attempt to erase God from everything there remains in the oceans and the seas wonderful examples that can only be explained by "When I consider Thy heavens, the work of Thy fingers, the moon and stars, which Thou hast ordained" (Psalm 8:3), and might I add the seas as well. Oh, that the scales would be removed from our eyes so that we might see the fashioning fingers of God and the handiwork of the hands of God, not only on the landscape and in the seascape, but in and around our own lives as well.

39.

BEACH BENEFITS

The Psalmist asked the thought provoking question, *"What shall I render unto the Lord for all His benefits toward me?"* (Psalm 116:12) We could focus our answer in a variety of categories, but in this book we are sharing, Sermonettes from the Seashore, my answer will be on the topic of beach benefits.

Whether Alison Point Beach in Valdez, Alaska, or Long Beach in LoveLadies, New Jersey, I have found one overriding benefit of beaches, and no, it isn't fishing. Whether Eilat Beach in Israel or Eve Beach in India, I have discovered what the human race has been acutely aware of since the first man walked a sandy shore. Whether Huntington Beach in California or Sandy Beach in Maine, I have learned that a few minutes or a few hours or even a few days by the ocean's edge can cure just about any aliment or illness of the mind or heart. I read in a book once that the British (a people who are surrounded by beaches) people have a saying that says, *"A few weeks by the sea will put it all right again."* I only came to understand this seaside concept when I took my burdens to the beaches of my life and found these benefits, benefits I recognize having come from the Creator of all beaches. So then, what are some of these beach benefits?

For me, the best beaches are those empty of people or having few people around. I know this can be rare, but I have been blessed numerous times with such a benefit. I shared in a few articles before about the day I spent on Alison Point Beach in Valdez, Alaska, fishing alone for hours just watching the grandeur of Valdez Bay and the variety of animal life there. That shoreline as does most shorelines has an atmosphere of serenity and solitude. The natural body is invigorated and stimulated by such places. The sea edge can restore weary limbs, revive strained emotions, and renew aching hearts. To breathe deeply salty air, to stretch bodily members in cooling breezes, and to look at wondrous sites and sights only brings a healing a beach can give. An ocean beach is not only a beautiful place to visit, but it also a beneficial place to be.

Most of us have experienced the benefits of salt water in the healing process, whether a little salt water for an aching throat or a little salt water to sterilize a sore or abrasion. Sometimes we put people with battered joints or sore ligaments in tubes of salty water or, if you have a chance or live by the sea, soaking in the ocean results in great relief. Add to that mixture a therapeutic sun and a warm breeze and you have the three main ingredients to full recovery from just about anything. That is why in years past, before the advent of the miracle medicines, people were sent to the ocean to be restored. Just walking by the sea and letting the ocean waves play against your feet was enough to start the healing. It cannot be calculated how many people over the centuries have been healed simply by being on a beach or near a sea, but most of us know it's true.

The Maker of sea and shore knew well when He created beaches that His grandest creation would need what those beaches could provide (no, not fish). God has always been the Great Healer. His Son proved that during His stay in Galilee. But more than a Personal Healer, the Almighty has placed within his creation means of healing. Mankind is discovering every day that in the rain forests of the Amazon there are healing properties in the plants and trees. Such has been the case for a trip to the beach or the ocean's edge when more than physical healing has come, the side benefit of a renewed spirit, a restored soul, a revitalized mind. One can find a variety of benefits on a beach, but don't miss the Creator of those benefits the next time you visit.

40.

TIDE THERAPY

It was on my very first trip to the gulf side of Florida that I learned the tremendous therapeutic value of the surf. I didn't understand at the time the scientific reason as I stood in the tides off Nokomis and Casperson Beaches. All I knew was I felt refreshed as the waves rolled over my winter-weary, pastorate-weary body. It wasn't until I returned to my home state of Maine and read the following by the internationally known naturalist, Phillip Keller that I began to see just how practical tidal therapy can be.

"Part of the reason that the sea possesses such potent healing properties is its content of a saline solution. It carries in suspension not only salt, but also a multitude of other trace minerals. Some of these rare substances are seldom found on land, yet they abound in the ocean. The fact that the sea waters which wash over the coastline in a continuous scouring action are salty tends to sterilize and cleanse the shore. The salt actually counteracts decay of materials that accumulate on the beach. It deters decomposition. It purifies and prevents undue putrefaction and pollution. The result is that the beach is not only beautiful to behold, but it is also a lovely place to be. There is a fragrance, a pungent freshness that permeates the air and quickens the senses. Part of this comes from the ozone off the sea. There is rich and abundant supply of oxygen in the breezes that blow in off the breakers. They are charged with moisture and trace elements that sweep in over the shore in potent stimulation. The sea water itself is a marvelous healing agent. Cuts, wounds, abrasions, sores, and skin blemishes are sterilized, cleansed, and enabled to heal with great rapidity. Even injured joints and torn ligaments, if bathed in the sea, then exposed to the warm therapy of the sun will mend in wondrous ways."

When Jesus would travel across the Sea of Galilee, sometimes the winds would pick up and the waves would build. On one such occasion recorded by Mark (It is my opinion that the Gospel According to Mark was actually the Gospel According to Peter because Peter and not Mark witnessed these events firsthand.) the disciples ventured across the sea only to be caught in a terrible sea storm. Jesus was asleep at first, but when he was awakened He commanded that the skies clear and the sea be still. After this came to pass the disciples asked this interesting question, "And they feared exceedingly, and said one to another, what manner of man is this, that even the wind and sea obey Him?" (Mark 4:41) Who of us is to know that the Almighty in His commands to the seas didn't instruct the waters and waves of the oceans to be a therapy, a tide therapy if you will? And to think that my Heavenly Father commanded the surf, sea, and sun to give me this sermonette. That is what the disciples missed that day as they struggled against that sea storm. The sea wasn't raging to hurt them, but to heal them. I believe Jesus took them into the sea to heal their fears about who He really was. Surely, the One that can command a sea storm to stop was who He said He was, the Son of God. For me, in the wave action off Nokomis and Casperson Beaches it was the healing of my minister's frustration and family concerns. By the time we arrived in Florida I had pastored three churches and had been in the work over twenty years. Most of them were blessed, but some of them burdensome. I learned as others before me had learned that a stroll along a sandy shore is therapeutic to body and soul, and that a dip into a raging sea can restore one's perspective on life and living. A contemplating swim in the sea renews one's faith in the greatness and grandeur of God, and that He was and still is the Master Healer of body and mind. Jesus was healing that day on the Galilee, and He was healing that day on Nokomis Beach.

41.

SURF SONG

As I sit before my computer screen, a raging north wind is blowing wildly around the Emmanuel Baptist Church on the coast of Maine. We have received our second major snow storm in ten days. With the eighteen inches we got yesterday and last night, our total for the last two storms is well over thirty inches. As I listen to the snow song playing outside, I am reminded of another song that used to play during a late winter snow on Moose Island where I pastored a few years ago, a surf song.

Jesus' brother Jude writes of ". . . raging waves of the sea . . ." (Jude 13) Thirty to forty mile-an-hour gusts would turn Passamaquoddy Bay into a raging sea. Few on this planet have had the privilege of hearing wind and wave play a duet together. Today outside my study window in Ellsworth I only hear the wind, but on a similar day in Eastport I would be enfolded with the melodies of snow, surf, wind, and waves in a quartet of sounds that would invigorate the senses. When my time was spent near the shore enjoying a simple afternoon break with a stroll on the seaside pier, I became lost in the natural music surrounding my small coastal city. I have always loved natural music versus manmade music. Despite the similarities at times, there is something quite calming in surf songs, stream songs, and cedar songs. Untouched by human hand, the ocean, even when raging, quiets the heart and quells the storm raging in one's head. The same has been for the songs of warblers, waterfalls, and wind chimes. A simple supplication is not lost in the music of the sea as it is at a modern concert, yes, for me, even too loud to pray. The symphony of surf, sea, and shore blend together in a trio of sounds that sooths the soul and makes the heart happy, like a wintry wind blowing snow up and down a shoreline.

The heavy, wet snow blankets the land to the water's edge. The wind makes great drifts and amazing patterns in the snow pack. Added to the creative waves pounding the seashore, the sights and sites are almost as wonderful as the music being created by the raging water and the roaring wind. Also unlike modern music this music is free. The heavenly Father has never charged admission to any one of His creation concerts. The sad truth that has come about today is that in these concerts most of the front rows are empty. Man would rather sit in a stuffy, smelly hall and listen to somebody tell a joke or try to sing a song. Few today take advantage of these wonderful tunes of nature, the top ten of nature's orchestras, or the songs of the seashore. On the days I ventured out to listen to God's radio and watch God's television, my neighbors were inside listen to man's radio and man's television and watching man's shows and listening to man's songs. Everybody was waiting for it all to end while I was enjoying the song that is only heard when snow and surf harmonized together.

My footprints track back from the shore as I head back to my study in the church building on Washington Street. My quiet interlude by the water's edge has inspired me again as this seventeenth snow of the season in Ellsworth inspired me to write this "sermonette from the seashore." As the waves of snow showers cover without, the roar from Passamaquoddy Bay covers within. The surf song has revitalized my soul and energized my spirit. As I walked the two blocks up from the harbor to the church, I felt again the peace of God that only comes with a song (Ephesians 5:19) and the admonition that only come from a hymn (Colossians 3:16). Only when we are tested in this way do we really hear the tune in the trouble, every attack an aria, and in every storm a surf song.

42.

SALMON STREAM

Around six o'clock in the evening of our only day in Valdez, Scott returned alone after getting his mother settled into our motel room. He had also taken her out to supper (two sandwich dinners for $40) before returning to see if his father had been eaten by bears. I must admit when he returned I was ready for a break (ten hour stretch of fishing), but not before fulfilling one of my Alaskan dreams of standing in a stream of salmon.

By the time Son returned I had fished every inch of Allison Point Beach. The tide had made a complete recovery, but because it hadn't reached the tree line I was able to cast my fly without getting caught in the branches and underbrush along the shore. Step by step and foot by foot I had worked my way along the shore until I came to a small stream that was flowing under the roadway through a culvert from a small creek that came out of the hillside just beyond the parking lot across the road from the beach. When I arrived at the brook I couldn't believe the number of salmon trying to swim up the shallow (barely a foot of water) stream. I walked out into the flow and kneeing down. Scott took a few photographs of me surrounded by salmon. They were all pink salmon (where were the silvers?), but it made a nice picture for my Alaskan fishing collection. It also reminded me of the prophecy of Ezekiel about the day the Dead Sea of Canaan will once again be teeming with fish. I travelled to the Dead Sea on a 2010 trip to Israel with my daughter Marnie and a group from Dallas Theological Seminary. I floated (you can't swim in the Dead Sea because of the density of salt and other minerals) in the Dead sea, but I spotted no fish or fishermen, yet Ezekiel foretells of a day, "And it shall come to pass, that the fishers shall stand upon it from Engedi [where we actually stopped to experience the Dead Sea] even unto Eneglaim; they shall be a place to spread forth nets; their fish shall be according to their kind [like at Alison Point Beach all pink salmon], as the fish of the great sea [talking of the Mediterranean Sea here, but the fish I was kneeling with were from the great sea we call the Pacific Ocean], exceeding many [I had never been with as many fish either at any one time]." (Ezekiel 47:10)

Working our way up the shore to the small stream that feeds a hatchery and eventually dumps into the bay at the head of the bay, I got to do something I had also dreamed about doing in Alaska, fishing with my hands. Since my boyhood I have been fishing and, yes, on a few occasions I have tried to catch a fish with my hands. What boy hasn't? The fish of which I speak were small minnows because no respectable fish would ever allow anyone to get close enough to be caught with hands, yet in Valdez that opportunity happened. I have photographical proof that I have done just that. The pink salmon were so thick in the stream by the hatchery that I literally stepped into the water, reached down, and started pulling four to seven pound salmon up out of the water with my hands. Scott stood on the shore with his camera as he took picture after picture of a half dozen salmon I picked up with my hands, but you can't really call it fishing. I had heard of fishing in a barrel, but this was easier than that. Perhaps, that is why I don't think my fishing in Valdez was really fishing. It was just plain too easy!

Scott and I returned to Allison Point and fished a couple more hours, but no silvers. We were back to the Best Western in Valdez by dark (10 o'clock), and it was nearly eleven before I was caught up in my journaling. Our ninth day in Alaska was over, and on the morrow we would be heading back to Fairbanks (one of our longest days on the road). I shut the light off, but I didn't go right to sleep. Who could after such a day on a beach?

43.

BEACH BIRD

Just in front of a small bridge that crossed the hatchery stream was a parking lot. We got out and decided to walk the beach on the bay side of the pink salmon hatchery. As we crawled down the small bank to the beach, we saw them—two huge bald eagles. That late afternoon and early evening was wrapped in August warmth, the air filled with seagulls soaring over the cliff behind us and the bay before us. The smell of dead fish was everywhere, yet at the same time the strong salty air gave off a fragrance that made the walk towards the eagles pleasant. The eagles we sought had landed at the seaside no doubt looking for a fresh meal. The seagulls on the other hand were looking for salmon eggs and fish eyes. One of my observations on my sea edge fishing trip was just how many of the dead fish on the shore had their eyes plucked out. Seagulls only eat what they like the best, and fish eyes were on their menu. The oddity of beach birds!

    Scott was determined to get a few up close and personal pictures of the eagles on the shore, but it wasn't long before Scott came too close and into the wind the pair went. At first they circled the sandy shore barely twenty feet in the air. I think they liked their fishing spot and didn't really want to leave, but our intrusion into their territory was bothering them. More often than not they set quietly and patiently waiting for the right time to liftoff, but when provoked by invaders like my son they are soon off into the one domain in which no enemy can follow, the wind. Ever since my first eagle sighting, I have been captivated by an eagle in the wind. With powerful strokes of their massive wings and despite their exceptional weight, it doesn't take an eagle very long to get into the air even from a sandy beach. Granted, taking off from a cliff or a tree is easier, but a flatland start is just as doable as it was that evening across the bay from Valdez. An eagle's takeoff starts with a shaking of itself, fluffing its plumage, and a lifting of its massive wings. (I judged the wings on the eagles were at least five-feet wide.) As with all other takeoffs I have witnessed over the years, the regal bird simple starts walking along the shore until enough air is under its wings for takeoff. Its only help was the slight breeze that was blowing up the bay that evening, yet within seconds the pair was flying over our heads heading for the cliff on the other side of the road.

Darkness was approaching and in the cool of the night the pair will rest on some old branch on the Lowe River or perhaps on a crag overlooking the hatchery. Whichever, I knew the eagles would be back the next day to fish and bulk themselves up for the long, cold Alaska winter. The glorious flight of any eagle (Jeremiah 49:22 "Behold, he shall come up and fly as the eagle . . .") is a cherished experience, but in Valdez that evening it was more special given the surroundings we were in. The last we saw of the pair of eagles in the wind was as they gained height and disappeared over the small ridgeline on the other side of the road. Their departure allowed Scott and me to continue our exploration of the stream by the hatchery. You might ask me why the eagles had taken so much of our attention when we were surrounded with the vastness of an Alaskan Bay. The answer is a simply one for me. In the wilds of Maine or the wilderness of Alaska I have yet to find any creature that has demanded my attention more than the bald eagle. Granted, if I were in India it would be different. In India I have had the privilege of seeing an Indian eagle that is much smaller than our eagle and in my opinion not as beautiful. They have a white head, yes, but more of a brownish body. Yet in that same park were white and royal Bengal tigers and of course Indian elephants, the best of the best! God has given man a variety of creatures to admire, but far above all we admire the Creator of those creatures!

44.

"EBB" EXPERIENCE

I woke in Valdez, Alaska, to a thick fog. It reminded me of my five years in a small, island community off the coast of Downeast Maine (Eastport on Moose Island). Coastal Maine has a climate and a culture all its own, but coastal island life is entirely different from the mainland (or as they say in Eastport "inland"), a way of life that can only be understood if you live there for a while or maybe a lifetime. If you're not from "there," then you will always have a hard time knowing why things are done as they are done and be accepted as one of them because, as the locals will tell you, it all has to do with the turning of the tide. "Surely your turning of things upside down shall be esteemed . . ." (Isaiah 29:16) is the Biblical concept but what of the practical precept?

The good Lord had once again been good to us on our tour of Alaska as our plans were to spend only one day in Valdez, and the day before the weather had been perfect. If we had come to Valdez a day later, we would have seen nothing because of the thickness of the fog. Our arrival on the twenty-first of August instead of the twenty-second made it possible for us to see the sites and sights in all of its majesty. The high mountains along the coastline create a small pocket of land for the residents of Valdez to live on. The Gulf of Alaska, and in particular the Bay of Valdez, cradles the citizens of Valdez in on the other side. The sheer size of the hills to the north and the sea to the south were scenic to say the least, the bigness of Alaska on display once again. Having lived in a similar town in Maine, I could understand the geography and topography as well as the attitude we found in Valdez. Its isolated, coastal living creates a self-reliant, hard-hearted, suspicious people. More often than not they will blame it all on the turning of the tide.

Yesterday I had spent most of my allotted time in Valdez fishing the tide of Valdez Bay hoping to land a "silver", (Coho) salmon, but to no avail. It was a mighty tide I felt on my waders because of the huge volume of water and the wide bay, but small (maybe twenty feet) compared to some I had experienced. The greatest tides in the world (averaging between 20-50 feet, but 70 feet at the mouth of the Petitcodiac River) are found in Fundy Bay (32 miles wide at its entrance and 96 miles long), New Brunswick, Canada. I have seen them up close and they are impressive. Even my little ministry town of Eastport has more spectacular tides (30 plus feet in places) in Passamaquoddy Bay than I witnessed in Valdez Bay, and though not all tides are created equal, there is something about the turning of the tide that affects those who live by its power, its timing, and its movements. So I had lived another day in my life under the influence of a strong tide. As I walked along the waterfront of Valdez on the morning of our departure, I felt it again. Despite the ocean fog that cut my visibility to a few hundred feet, I could sense the moving of the sea. I like to explain it like the ocean taking a breath. Exhaling is the outgoing tide and inhaling is the incoming tide. It is at that moment of transition that the tide turns.

That turning is called "the ebb." The laws of the sea are quite simple and there comes a time, the lowest time, when a dramatic change is going to happen. It is hard to see, it is so subtle, but the ebb is the turning point when the tide takes charge again. Its rhythm is so regular and so reassuring that its pattern and process can be timed and clocked to the exact second because the lowest ebb of the sea is the turning of the tide. I stood gazing out into the fog of Valdez Bay, and I thought we too had come to the "ebb" of our trip. We had reached as far as we would go in Alaska, and it was time to head back to Fairbanks. Six days on the road and it was time to finish the circle and like the tide return to the place we had started. Life itself will have such ebbs, and little did my son know that he was in the ebb of his life as he left the regular army for the reserves, but what he didn't realize and what his mother and I didn't realize this would be his last ebb!

45.

VALDEZ VISTA

At the writing of this remembrance of our time spent in Valdez, I have just finished a wonderful devotion by Vance Havner under the title of "turn of the tide" in which he gives a marvellous application to the precept of the tide. He writes, "The lowest ebb is the turn of the tide. It is true of more than the ocean. We have an old proverb that says just about the same thing: *'The darkest hour is just before the dawn.'* We have seen it happen again and again. Maybe it was a crisis in serious illness. Someone almost died, then came a turn. The patient touched bottom and then started up. Or it was low ebb in the family fortune or failure in a career. Everything was lost, we thought, but no, when everything was darkest, came the dawn . . . Civilization stands today at low ebb. Never has there been such scientific advancements, such material wealth, such intellectual brilliance, but the soul of humanity is sick. America flies the skies, but also flounders in the slime. Such low ebb does not guarantee a turn of the tide, however, for history does not operate like the ocean. Nations die, civilizations rot, and kingdoms pass away. We learn from history that nobody learns history. The world is awash today in tidal waves of revolution. Other lands are surging in worldwide ferment. There is no certainty that our American low ebb means a turn in the tide. The church is at low ebb today. Religious leaders wring their hands and beat their breasts. Of course there have been low ebbs before . . . but this does not justify such a state. God never intended it. Low ebb and high tide are orderly processes of nature but Christianity was never meant to fluctuate up and down. There is no justification for 'malarial' Christians, living from fever to chill. Low-grade religion is a consequence of sin. However, there will be an incoming tide of some sort one of these days. Will it be our Lord's return? Or revival? Or retribution? One thing is certain, *the tide never stays out!* And the lowest ebb is the turn of that tide . . . And Jeremiah in his fifth lamentation turned from a dark picture of the times as pen can write, to say, 'Turn thou us unto Thee, O Lord, and we shall be turned; renew our days as of old.' (Lamentations 5:21) With him the lowest ebb was the turn of the tide."

Truly we live in an age where the fog is so thick we can't see clearly, but despite our lack of vision the tide is turning. I find it fascinating that even while on vacation the spiritual side of me is always looking for a lesson, a teaching, or an instruction into something more important than a day fishing the tide with a Valdez vista. I think now I see why the Lord gave me and my family such a day. Another day living with the turning of the tide, another day experiencing the ebb tide, whether the ocean ebb, trip ebb, or just maybe, Scott's ebb. One of the reasons my wife and I took this trip was to be with our son as he, too, came to an ebb time in his life. The military life he had known for eight years was over. A new tide in his life was beginning, and we wanted to be there to encourage him and help where we could as he made the transition back into civilian life. Such swings in one's life are not always easy, and the surge and redirection can be daunting and dangerous. We know that Scott has been in an ebb time in his spiritual life for a long time. It was and still is our prayer that even though he might be at his lowest, that the tide isn't still going out and the turn has happened. As with any ebb tide, it takes a while to see the change. As I fished Allison Point I couldn't tell exactly when the ebb passed and the tide started to come in, but as the afternoon passed I did notice the tree line coming closer and closer as I moved with the tide up the shoreline. So it is with life. My prayer is that we are in a turning time, a transition time. We were!

46.

WASHING WAVES

For the first time in my life, I had time to sit, ponder, and meditate on the meaning of the washing of the waves on a beach.

My wife Coleen and I were vacationing in Nokomis, Florida, with a couple from the Emmanuel Baptist Church, our church in Ellsworth, Maine. Being our first time in Florida, it took Coleen and me a few days to discover the joys of a sandy beach in the middle of January. All week the weather was perfect for a seashore hike, seashell harvesting, and shark's teeth hunting. Our hosts had driven us up to Casperson Beach for all three "firsts." I will never forget the grandeur of the Gulf the first time I saw the Gulf of Mexico in all its glory because as far as the eye could see there was sea, unlike most of the coast of Maine where your view of the Atlantic Ocean has an island or two blocking the broad view. The same was true of the beach at Casperson, up and down as far as your eye could focus was nothing but sand. The sand was warm and clean. I don't think I expected to see any trash, but there were no manmade materials of any kind along the shoreline. It was a lovely place to stroll in your bare feet.

As I broke off from my companions, I walked slowly through the surf looking for shark's teeth. I was not a collector, but the exercise opened my eyes to the actions of the waves crashing on shore. Foam covered waves combed the shore every few seconds. You could dig a hole, as I did, and within a few waves the sand was void of the imprint I made. The scar I had made in the seashore was completely erased. It wasn't long before I realized just why the beach was clear of any debris. The rolling breakers were constantly at work washing the shore of anything that was out of place on the pristine beach. With each wave, the shoreline was scrubbed and scoured by the salty sea. Nothing was allowed to remain on the beach for very long, and what the sea didn't take the beachcomber took. Though the heavier objects resisted at first, all eventually yielded to the magnificent process of the waves.

I watched as the waves moved quietly over the beach. (It was a calm day in the Gulf that day.) Once the power of the wall of water reached it maximum reach, its watery fingers pulled back again. In its grip was anything that had polluted that section of shore. In order not to be pulled back into the sea, small creatures like shrimp had to burrow into the sand. Even the seagulls and terns didn't venture far into the surf least they be pulled into the water. I learned that day on Casperson Beach that the waves were carrying out a perpetual process of cleaning. The outpouring power of the surf was to sterilize the shoreline from all that would pollute. The washing waves played no favorites to any creature or object caught in its path. It cleared away all garbage and in time carried it away out to sea. The waves saw all objects on its shore as filth. With meticulous care the washing waves cleansed the coast at Casperson.

As I watched this amazing process unfold on the coast of Florida, I pondered an equally powerful process in the spiritual realm and that being the cleansing power of the Word of God. Paul wrote to the Ephesians, "That he might sanctify and cleanse it with the washing of water by the Word." (Ephesians 5:26) Paul was talking about the power of the Word on the Church or the saint of God. God's intent is for us to allow the Bible's cleaning waves (verses) to roll over us on a daily basis just like the waves on Casperson Beach. Exposed to the Word, the cleaning process will carry away all sin, wickedness, and evil in our lives. When was the last time you were washed by a wave of the Word?

47.

TITANIC THRUST

One of the things I learned on my winter trip to Florida was that there are no two days alike on the seashore. One day the Gulf of Mexico was as peaceful as a northern Maine lake on a calm day. On another day the Gulf of Mexico was as troubled as that same northern Maine afternoon gale. It was on that day I experienced my first ocean thrust, a titanic thrust in every sense of the word.

Both days, the calm day and the cauldron day, were bathed in a brilliant sun and white sand. On that second day we were facing a gathering storm far out to sea, but the waves were warning of its approach. The wind was up, but still pleasantly warm. The surf was up as well with roaring waves higher than my height, and I stand a good six feet! The Psalmist was right when he wrote, "Let the heavens rejoice, and let the earth be glad; let the sea roar, and the fullness thereof." (Psalm 96:11) My first day on the beach I walked without effort through the small rolling surf, but on that last day in Florida I couldn't keep my balance in the walls of waves that engulfed me every few seconds. It was when I stood firm and faced those oncoming waves of water that I felt the gigantic grip of the sea and the titanic thrust of the ocean.

As I waded into the rising surf, I wondered why so few were swimming. That day the beach at Nokomis was crowded with "snowbirds," but few if any of them were in the water. I looked back as I ventured deeper into the surf and saw some of my fellow vacationers looking for seashells while others were simply sunning themselves. Along the seawall a few were fishing, while an equal number were simply strolling up and down the sandy beach. A few that were reading along the shore would on occasion look up from their books no doubt wondering and puzzled as this "white" northerner slowly stepped deeper into the Gulf. I know some probably thought I was crazy given the cooler water and the strengthening surf, soon to be sunburned, or salt burned, or caught in a rip current. Most were already bronzed, but I hadn't been there long enough. Besides, this was my last day, and a tough winter was still raging on the coast of Maine so I was going to enjoy the warm water to the last. I was determined that if I never made the trip again (and I haven't), I could always boast that I had at least taken one plunge into a storm tossed sea.

As my wife Coleen and our friends the Clarks looked on, I jumped and splashed in the large breakers smashing onto Nokomis Beach. Despite nearing fifty, I acted like a foolish kid yelling and laughing as the waves pounded me into the surf. I would come up spitting saltwater, waiting for the next titanic thrust to pick me up from off my feet and throw me forward with a mighty push. As my feet left the sandy bottom I was carried toward shore with ease. I don't know how many tons of water rolled over me that afternoon, but each was a thrill. Man has tried to duplicate that experience in his water parks, but no human ride can match the power and the pleasure created when wind and wave combine just offshore on a Florida beach. Sea spray in my eyes and saltwater in my mouth only brought me out of the surf for a few minutes, then I was back in for another plunge and another pull waiting with anticipation and expectation for another untamed titanic thrust.

As my wife and friends watched me struggle in the surf so too does our Friend (Proverbs 18:24) watch us as the waves of life roll over us in the deeper parts of living. Overshadowing the storm on the horizon is the overseeing eye of our Father. He will always give us the surf, sea, and sand to enjoy before the storm and, as the hymn writer put it, "A shelter in a time of storm." (Hebrews 13:5-6)

48.

OCEAN ORGAN

In the main sanctuary (the old church structure actually had two, one on the upper level and one on the lower level) of the old Washington Street Baptist Church in Eastport, Maine, where I once had a pastorate for five years, there was located an ancient pipe organ with an exceptional sound. (When the church building was sold and a new church building built, the old organ was still so valuable that it was bought by a church in Australia, taken apart piece by piece, and shipped halfway around the world.) The organ was well over a hundred years old, and when I was there, this organ thrilled my soul each and every time I heard it played. Being unmusical, I had to rely on the God-given abilities of others to enjoy the notes and tones that came from that amazing organ. I wasn't very long in Eastport before I found another organ in Moose Island that only God could play. David wrote in his psalms that we are to ". . . praise Him with . . . organs." (Psalm 150:4) Every time I read of David's admonition, I am reminded of the pipe organ of the Washington Street Baptist Church and the ocean organ of Passamaquoddy Bay.

Helen Boone (at the compiling of this sermonette Helen has just passed into glory) was the organist of the church when I first moved to Moose Island. She was also the caretaker of the organ. Her father had once been the man who pumped the billows by hand before the process was electrified sometime midway through the twentieth century. The organ was slow to the touch because each note was controlled by wooden reeds making the touch on the keys to the opening of the pipes delayed. It took some getting use to for the organist, but the heavenly sound was worth the wait. Despite her devoted care of the organ, Helen was not beyond letting others play the valued instrument. I still remember the time a good friend of mine, Charles Nason, played the organ for me. The tall, lanky music teacher worked the key and then the peddle with such precision! I could only sit in the back of the sanctuary absorbing every note into my inner soul. When I had family and friends visit that could play, like my sister Sylvia, I would provoke them to play the organ. Each time I walked upstairs into that grand hall at the church, I wished I could play the organ, but like the ocean organ off shore, others had to play.

More often than not each and every time I would walk out to Shackerford's Head I could hear God's organ sound. Unlike the church organ, this ocean organ could only be played by the Almighty. With the breeze for air and the sea and surf for the pipes, the songs and sounds that came from the bay and brush were heavenly to my ears. As I would sit and listen to Helen or Charles in the church sanctuary, I would sit on the bluff overlooking Passamaquoddy Bay and listen intently to God's music. There on that hilltop I realized that David's organs (I don't know if it was the same instrument) were plural, manmade and God-made. I believe He would have us listen to both and use both to praise Him and glorify His Son Jesus Christ.

So often is the case with the music of the human organ, the organ that God has put within each and every one of us. I have been singing all my life these words from the hymn writer, "Down in the human heart, crushed by the temper, feelings lie buried that grace can restore; touched by a loving heart, wakened by kindness, chords that are broken will vibrate once more." In response to this I like what Vance Havner wrote on August 23, 1936, "Mine you, we never were meant to be the organists of our soul. We cannot play but we are the custodians; we can let Jesus play or refuse Him. All the trouble in human lives begins when the custodian tries to be the organist!" As I let Helen play the church organ and God the ocean organ, so must I allow Christ to play the organ of my soul.

49.

HANDYMAN HANDIWORK

The Psalmist speaks of "the heavens declare the glory of God; and the firmament sheweth His handywork." (Psalm 19:1) I don't know what I would have done over all these years (44 now) at the church building or the parsonage if it were not for the handymen of the churches (four of them) I have pastored. I tell people all the time that my hands are the most useless members of my body, and poor is the church that has to rely on me to fix anything. This reality came clearly into focus during my third pastorate where the church building had been around for over 150 years, a church structure that was in constant need of care and correcting. When I arrived in 1986, I not only inherited an old structure, but a superior handyman in Fred Boone.

Call him a custodian, a janitor, a caretaker, a sexton, whatever. Fred Boone was an odd job specialist. He kept all the machinery in the church working, from the furnace to the fixtures. He was an electrician, a plumber, a painter, and a gardener. A product of Moose Island, Fred took an early retirement from a Pratt & Whitney plant in Connecticut to return home to Eastport to take care of his dying mother. The building of the Washington Street Baptist Church was also dying with age, and it was Fred's seaside firmament.

Handyman Fred mowed the grass, found lost articles left by the Sunday school kids, repaired the furniture, cleaned up after the church suppers, oiled the squeaky doors, helped in the kitchen, filled the baptistery when needed, fixed the constantly leaking roof and the leaks coming from the decaying bell tower, plastered the falling walls, and when anything broke he fixed it. Much of what Fred did in the old building wasn't under his job description, but he did it anyway. Fred was one of those church members I found hard to say what department he work in because it seemed that he worked in all the departments of the church. It came down to this simple truth. Fred loved the Lord, and he loved the church. His was always ". . . a work of faith, and a labor of love, and a patience of hope . . ." (I Thessalonians 1:3) Fred was any pastor's dream worker.

Oh, the church had a pastor (me), a deacon and trustee board, a Sunday school department, a social committee, and youth leaders, but despite these well-meaning helpers, the services and programs would have ground to a halt if it hadn't been for Mr. Fix-it because of just how bad the church building was in ill repair. Most of the time nobody knew that Fred was even around, but when you needed a hand or the church needed a repair, Fred was always there seemingly always on call. Most of the time he had the right tool to fix-it, change it, or replace it. In the church basement, or should I say the hole under the church that Fred had dug out with his own hands, Fred had every tool imaginable. What he didn't have there he had in his car. Despite the rambling church structure, Fred chose a place for his stuff that wouldn't interfere with any church function. That was Fred, a silent-in-the-shadows servant; the Handyman's (God) handyman, a man much like his Lord and Saviour Jesus Christ.

Living in Eastport for five years, I had a chance to see much of God's handiwork in the shoreline and seascape off Moose Island and in Passamaquoddy Bay. As I saw God's "handiwork," I was reminded that His Son was placed in a handyman's home (Mark 6:3), and I am persuaded that Jesus became a handyman as well. I know a church must move on at the death of a handyman, but I praise the Lord to this day that Fred didn't pass on my watch. I shudder to think what might have happened if he had (Fred has since gone on to glory). I believe handymen move to the front of the line when they move from earth to heaven. Don't you.

50.

"LIFE" LESSON

"*And God said, Let the waters bring forth abundantly the moving creature that hath life . . . And God created great whales, and every living creature that moveth, which the waters brought forth abundantly, after their kind . . . and God blessed them, saying, Be fruitful, and multiply, and fill the waters in the seas . . .*" (Genesis 1:20-22) There is only one seashore that I have visited that didn't exhibit life and that was the shores of the Dead Sea in a 2010 trip with my daughter Marnie. Every other shoreline was a lesson in life.

Any walk along the ocean's edge will convince any stroller that the waters of this planet have fulfilled God's creative command of "abundantly." I have visited beaches and seas all over this world and other than the exception I illustrated above, I have found an abundance of sea life. Everywhere you turn both at the water's edge or on the water you see life, life, and more life. There is not only an abundance of marine life, but the creature we call "bird" is also in abundance, the other creature in which God gave life on the fifth day (Genesis 1:23). Whether mammals in the surf, birds in the air, or fish in the sea, the oceans are full of life. Invisible at times this abundance of life will reveal itself if one is patient, whether dolphins off Nokomis Beach in Florida, bluefish off the Jersey shore, otters and sea lions off California, or whales in Passamaquoddy Bay. As one strolls along any shore and watches the setting sun, that burning, bright orb falling into the sea, there is that overriding sense of life, abundant life, all around you.

This life comes from a trio of seagulls drifting in the ocean's sea breeze above the water. Eventually you watch as they light on the sandy shore before you looking for a meal from the surf. Just off shore you might see the pelicans, a few terns, and maybe even a cormorant also looking for supper in the surf. If your eyesight is sharp, you might even see a school of small fish break the surface of the sea and then the attack of the winged predators. If you are really fortunate, you might pass a shore fisherman as he pulls in the catch-of-the-day, a sea bass, a striper, or the mighty blue fish. Everywhere you look and in each experience the oceans and the sea reveal the abundance of life within. And then there are on the beach and tidal pools signs of crab and sea worms coming and going with the tide. One of our favorite walks is along a rocky Maine coast beach in search of sea glass, but without fail we always find some kind of life as well.

Every rise of the tide will bring with it life, and even when you see no life there is that microscopic plankton, the world's greatest food source for both the ocean creatures and a great source of protein for human life. Add to that the seaweed which Maine has plenty and thousands of kinds of ocean plants, and the world's waters are teeming with life. Both the creatures and the plants are the wonderful web of life the Divine Designer put in the seas to sustain life both in the waters and in the lands of the world. When will mankind realize the daily gifts of life by God Himself? As the sun sets at the end of every seashore walk and you breathe that final breath of salty air, there ought to be one lesson left in your brain, one final instruction in your mind, one lasting teaching in your head, that being the "life" lesson. Each day new life is born in the sea, and each day fresh life comes from the sea. In that life is the life of this planet and at the heart of that life is the Almighty, the author or life. John would write this of Jesus. "In Him was life; and the life was the light of men." (John 1:4) Whether on the seashore, above the seashore, or in the sea, God gives us plenty of examples of life.

51.

DIFFICULT DECISION

I walked slowly into the back room of the Washington Street Baptist Church in Eastport, Maine. I turned on the small space heater, but I knew from experience it would be hours before the room would be comfortable. Oh, the air around me would immediately warm fast, but the steel desk and wooden chair would warm excruciatingly slow. They were cold, and I was freezing, but this was my place of decision, and I knew I had to endure until the answer came to me. I felt like the ancient Hebrew prophet Joel, "Multitudes, multitudes in the valley of decision; for the day of the Lord is near in the valley of decision." (Joel 3:14) But instead of a valley, I was by the seaside.

My church office was a large room in the back corner of the downstairs of a Baptist church on an island off the downeast coast of Maine. There was a tiny furnace that heated the room, but in the spring and fall I hated to turn it on. I have always been like that, trying to save the church a few bucks. The place had to warm from scratch each morning, and when it was barely 40 degrees outside and sleeting, it took a while. The problem that morning was it wasn't only sleeting outside, but there was a spiritual sleet inside my office as well. My soul was experiencing a seaside storm of epic proportions. I had been called into the pastorate in 1967, educated and graduated from my studies in 1973, interned and ordained into three pastorates before 1991. I knew what I was: a small town pastor. I know what to do in small-town Maine, but was it time to leave? The call had come from a city church, but I wasn't sure it was my calling. I was cold, afraid, knowing a wrong choice would put not only my ministry in danger, but my family in peril. I have watched others in my profession make wrong choices and the devastating results to family and church. I was spiritually shivering, and I couldn't stop shaking. The sea around Moose Island was cold that day, very cold, but not as cold as my heart!

It was nearly springtime, my second favorite season of the year (fall is the best), but my heart was as cold as a mid-winter day in the County (Aroostook County, the land of my birth). I couldn't seem to warm up physically or spiritual that morning as I pondered the most important decision of the year, and maybe my life (as it turned out to be the last major ministerial move of my life). It was too cold to study or read, and my meditation felt like frostbite. What was I going to do? My family of three seemed all keen to move to the big city of Ellsworth in Hancock County, a hundred miles farther down the coast of Maine. I was the only one dragging my feet, but the decision was ultimately mine and mine alone. And I was as uncertain as the sleet outside the walls of my study not knowing whether to rain or snow. Should I go or stay, a simple choice, a small decision, yet difficult for me that morning.

I sat in my cold chair behind my cold desk trying to thaw out my cold thoughts. I wanted to minister in "the county" (back home), but that door closed on me the year before. I loved the peace and quiet of Eastport, but I knew my gifts for helping the church had run out months before. I was in a spiritual Arctic wasteland, snow blind, with no direction or destination visible. The storm battering the coastline and seascape of Moose Island was equal to the spiritual storm battering my mind and soul. As the morning lengthened and my study began to warm a bit, so did my thoughts. It was then the small voice inside began to take my focus off the cold and settle it on the warmth that no matter here or there, God would be here or there with me. I realized again it was not the people but the place God wanted me that would be the best for me and my family. The best part of the Eastport flock, my family, I was taking with me to another seaside.

52.

ONE OCEAN

It wasn't until I read these lines by Phillip Keller that I learned of the oneness of the ocean. *"There are some aspects of the ocean that twentieth century technology has opened up to our understanding with tremendous interest. One of these great discoveries is that all water of all the oceans is in fact one gigantic fluid. It is in constant motion and movement, circulating by means of colossal currents from pole to pole and clear around the earth. The ancient idea that each ocean or great inland sea, such as the Mediterranean, was more or less a self-contained body of water, restricted roughly within its own continental basin and boundaries, is no longer valid. We know for a fact that these great oceans actually flow unto one another in gigantic subsurface rivers that make the Mississippi, Nile, and Amazon seems like mere trickles in comparison."*

This has helped me to understand why so often in Scripture "the sea" is mentioned and not "seas." Nahum in his contrasting Nineveh with the Nile and Egypt wrote, "Art thou better than populous No, that was situate among the rivers, that had the waters round about it, whose rampart was the sea, and her wall was the sea?" (Nahum 3:8) Nahum's analogy speaks of rivers, waters, and the sea, but not seas. The Psalmist also takes up this theology with these words, "He gathereth the waters of the sea together as an heap: He layeth up the depth in storehouses." (Psalm 33:7) Note again, waters, but a singular sea. I have checked numerous Biblical references, and this concept that Keller writes about is clearly seen in the Word of God.

Interestingly, another scientific reality long taught in God's Holy Writ which is just beginning to be understood by the scientific community, just beginning to be accepted by mankind as truth. Mankind has always been slow in accepting the Bible at face value, but once again technology and tests have proven the Creator right again in His scientific papers found in the Bible.

So what could be the lesson the good Lord would have us learn by this scientific discovery? For me, the sermonette by the seashore teaches me the oneness of God. Man has always wanted to believe in the plurality of gods, like his belief in the oceans, separate beings, interacting, but distinct. The Greeks and the Romans had panoply of gods as have most people groups scattered around the world, and even modern man is trying again to join all the gods of all the religions into one happy family of gods. But the Bible clearly states, "Hear, O Israel: the Lord our God is one Lord." (Deuteronomy 6:4) Even the New Testament, through the pen of Paul, states clearly, "One God and Father of all, who is above all, and through all, and in you all." (Ephesians 4:6) As with only one ocean there is no room for another and with one God and one Lord there is no room for others. All this talk and debate about the makeup of the sea has now been put to rest as should the talk and debate about other gods. The good Lord put within the handiwork of His creation a perfect illustration of the oneness of God. A careful study will reveal that God loves to deal in ones because Paul wrote in the context of the One God, "There is one body, and one Spirit, even as ye are called in one hope of your calling; one Lord, one faith, one baptism!" (Ephesians 4:4-5) So it should not surprise us that the God of oneness would put this concept of Himself in more than one doctrine. So the one ocean precept is just another way for God to point back to Himself in His creative work in the waters of the world when on the third day God said, "Let the waters under the heaven be gathered together into one place . . ." (Genesis 1:9)

53.

SALT SEA

Our trip (Israel May, 2010) from Masada took us up Route 90 another ten miles. By eleven o'clock we were stopping at a tourist center for lunch and a dip in the Dead Sea (Biblically called the salt sea in Joshua 3:16, "... and those came down toward the sea of the plain, even the salt sea ..."). It was not until after we left the Dead Sea that I found we had stopped at the Biblical site of En Gedi (one of my great disappointments of the trip).

En Gedi, like Hebron and Petra, was one of the places I really wanted to visit on our Israeli tour. I had seen the wonderful pictures of the spring of En Gedi and the oasis David found there in his wilderness wandering from King Saul (I Samuel 24:1). (Some believe that David wrote his 57th Psalm from there.) It was in a cave not far for where we had stopped that David saved Saul's life for a second time (I Samuel 24:2-15). I wanted to experience for myself "the spring of the goat" (En Gedi), the two beautiful waterfalls (Nahal David and Nahal Arugot), and perhaps see the amazing array of wildlife (the Ibex is known for haunting the area) that it draws to the spring that never runs dry (just like the Gihon Spring). The first mention of this oasis in this bleak and barren land is in Genesis 14:7. It is called Hazezon-Tamar or the "row of palms" in the story of the kings of the east invading the city states (like Sodom) along the Dead Sea. II Chronicles 20:2 tells us that Hazezon-Tamar and En Gedi are one and the same. After the heat and dust of Masada, I, like David, wanted to enjoy the lush vegetation and the cooling waters that was En Gedi. To finish off my Masada experience I wanted to see where the slaves of Silva carried the water that quenched the thirst of the legion that conquered Masada. I wanted to work my way through the narrow entrance that separated the tropical paradise of En Gedi from the torturous landscape that was the Dead Sea, but instead of the refreshing waters of En Gedi our group leader and tour guide chose for us to experience the bitter waters of a dead lake, a salt sea.

    After another terrible lunch that cost a fortune, Marnie and I got ready with the rest of our group to experience the waters of the Dead Sea. Don't get me wrong concerning what I have already written because you must remember I didn't know just how close we were to En Gedi so I was excited to witness for myself the impossibility of sinking in the Dead Sea. As we changed into our bathing suits, we realized that our stay in the water would have to be short. Both Marnie and I are fair-skinned, and we burn very easily. It was over 100 degrees when we stepped out of the dressing rooms about 300 yards from the shore of the Dead Sea. The walk to the seashore revealed what we were up against. It was hot, not humid, but a very dry, overpowering heat. The Sea we were getting ready to sit in (you don't jump in because it is important you keep the water out of your eyes so you simply back into the water and sit down) was at the lowest point on the planet, 1279 feet below sea level (for a contrast Death Valley in California is only 282 feet below sea level). We were nearly half-way down the western shore of the Dead Sea which is 48 miles long and 10 miles wide, and in the northern basin the water can reach a depth of 1300 feet. We would see through the haze of the heat at mid-day the Jordanian Plateau on the eastern shore. Land locked and without any outlets, the water from the Jordan River (and as I learned after our float, the waters of En Gedi as well) flows into the sea but only through evaporation does any water leave the sea. The high levels of salt and other minerals create a buoyancy resulting in a swimmer's inability to sink. The deadness of this sea versus the life in other seas is a wonderful contrast between mankind and the Almighty.

54.

STERILE SEA

A little after noon on May 21, 2010, Marnie was the first to back into the Dead Sea and sit down. I took a few pictures of her bobbing around before I followed her example. What I found the most strange was the difficulty I had trying to get my feet down. Sure enough, you actually feel like you are sitting in a recliner with the footrest up. To keep you in an upright position seemed at first complicated because I felt like I would roll over. The only way to keep from flopping over was to get your feet down in the water to act as a rudder. In my first tries I simply couldn't force my legs to sink. Only when I realized I had to tuck my legs close to my body was I able to drive them into the water. I was surprised just how clear the water was. Even twenty feet off shore you could see the rocks on the bottom clearly. The water had a milky look to it compared to the perfectly clear water of a Grand Lake Stream in Maine but clear enough to see deep into the Dead Sea. There was a slight sulfurous odor in the air as we enjoyed the sensation of floating in "a thick, warm, tub of salty soup" as one commentator put it. We floated and bobbed around for about fifteen minutes. I had given my camera to Ike Spiker, and he recorded our brief swim. I tried to get Marnie to cover herself in the black mud (lots of people come to the Dead Sea just to cover themselves in what they believe to be the healing agents found in the minerals in the mud) of the sterile sea, but her skin was already itching from the salt (Joshua 12:3), a taboo to Marnie.

I did get some pictures of other people caked in mud as we waited to wash the salt of the sea off our body by the fresh water showers. It was then I learned that the water we were using to wash ourselves off came from the spring of En Gedi. So we first showered on the shore and then walked back to the changing rooms to shower again. Marnie and I literally threw away our bathing suits and anything else we wore in the Dead Sea because the chemicals were that strong. After getting cleaned up, we returned to the picnic area and shared our impressions with the rest of the group. Most took the opportunity to experience the Dead Sea, but some just relaxed before our journey continued. About mid-afternoon we left En Gedi for Qumran, the home of the famous Dead Sea scrolls.

It was only after I returned to Maine and was pondering my disappointments and delights at the Dead Sea at En Gedi that I discovered Ezekiel 47:6-11. Read these verses carefully and then consider the amazing prophecy that is being predicted there. The Dead Sea will one day be fresh water, and it will be filled with fish like the Mediterranean (means "middle of the earth") Sea (the Bible calls this sea "the sea of the Philistines" Exodus 23:31, "the sea" Numbers 13:29, "the uttermost sea" Deuteronomy 11:24, or in our key verse printed above "the great sea" Numbers 34:6). It says that the fishermen will spread their nets in En Gedi. I didn't see any fishermen at En Gedi, just swimmers. What this promise tells me is that there is hope for the most desolate. There is hope for the dead, and that we serve a God who is able to restore even a dead sea to life. As I thought on this concept I was reminded of these verses from the pen of Joel the prophet,

"And I will restore to you the years that the locust hath eaten, the cankerworm, and the caterpillar, and the palmerworm, my great army which I sent among you. And ye shall eat in plenty, and be satisfied, and praise the name of the Lord your God that hath dealt wondrously with you: and my people shall never be ashamed. And ye shall know that I am in the midst of Israel, and that I am the Lord your God." (Joel 2:25-27) I look forward to the day when I will fish rather than float in the Dead Sea.

55.

SEA SUNSET

The Sea of Galilee is a freshwater lake fed primarily by the flow of the Jordan River which enters the lake between Bethsaida and Capernaum on the north shore. The river exits on the southern shore continuing its travel until it finally empties into the Dead Sea.

The lake is 680 feet below sea level making it the lowest freshwater lake in the world, and like its bigger brother, the Dead Sea, the Sea of Galilee is called by a number of names in the Bible: *Tiberius (John 6:1), Gennesaret (Luke 5:1), and Chinnereth (Numbers 34:11)*. The lake was on the very rich trade caravan route that ran both along the King's Highway on the eastern shore, and the Via Maris which passed on the north shore. Josephus, the Jewish historian during the time of Jesus, tells us that about 40,000 people lived around the shore and that 2300 boats (one was Peter's) fished the lake. He also wrote this: "Now this lake of Gennesaret is so called from the country adjoining it. Its breadth is forty furlongs and its length one hundred and forty. Its waters are fresh, and very agreeable for drinking. The country that lies over against this lake has the same name of Gennesaret; its nature is wonderful as well as its beauty; its soil is so fruitful that all sorts of trees can grow upon it, and the inhabitants accordingly plant all sorts of trees there; for the temper of the air is well mixed, that it agrees very well with those types, particularly walnuts, that require the coldest air. There are palm trees also, which grow best in hot air; fig trees and olive grow near them, which require an air that is more moderate. One may call this place the ambition of nature, where it forces those plants that are naturally enemies to one another to agree together, it is a happy contention of the seasons, as if every one of them laid claim to this country, for it not only nourishes different sorts of autumnal fruit beyond men's expectation, but preserves them a great while; it supplies men with the principal fruits, with grapes and figs continually, during ten months of the year, and the rest of the fruits as they become ripe together through the whole year; for besides the good temperature of the air, it is also watered from a most fertile fountain [the Jordan River]." We found this two thousand year old description as accurate on May 24, 2010, as during our three day stay on or near its seashore.

We arrived at the resort just before seven. We checked into our private cabin, went to supper, and then just before sunset put on our swim suits for our first of three dips into the warm waters of the Sea of Galilee. Marnie and I were the first ones to take the plunge. Less than a hundred yards from the front door of our bungalow was the shoreline of the lake. Directly across the lake we could see the lights of Tiberius, and there just to the right of the lights were the Cliffs of Arbel. Each night we were there, the sun sat directly over the cliffs. The sight was divine, but to witness the setting of the sun from the waters of the lake was heavenly. The water was the warmest lake water I had ever experienced (only cold water lakes in Maine), and the wind was blowing just enough to create small wavelets. Marnie and I made our first pilgrimage to the water just as the sun touched the Arbel Cliffs. The rule at the resort was no swimming in the dark. We only had about a half an hour that first night, but thirty minutes was enough to satisfy the urge we had upon our first sighting of Jesus' Sea. As we walked the rocky, sandy beach to the water's edge all we could remember were these lines from Matthew 4:18, "And Jesus, walking by the Sea of Galilee, saw . . ." Now we too had walked by that same sea and had seen what Jesus had seen from the shore of the world's most famous lake. What a thrill to not only walk the paths of Jesus, but to see what He saw—a sea sunset.

56.

GALILEE GALLEON

"*After these things Jesus went over* THE SEA OF GALILEE, *which is the Sea of Tiberias.*" (John 6:1) I have mentioned before that one of the thrills of traveling through Israel in 2010 was the opportunity to do Biblical things such as riding a camel, walking through a water tunnel, drawing water from a cistern, riding a donkey, picking stones from Elah brook, drinking water from Harod Stream, and taking a boat ride across the Sea of Galilee from the western shoreline to the eastern seashore.

We boarded our tourist boat (sometimes called a pilgrim boat but I called it our "Galilee galleon") from a dock just behind the Yigal Allon Center. Other than a few other boats similar to ours, there was very little activity on the lake. I remember reading this once from the pen of George Adam Smith about the Sea of Galilee: "*Where there are now no trees there were great woods; where there are marshes, there were noble gardens, where there is but one boat, there were fleets of sails!*" Certainly the Sea of Galilee has changed since the days Peter plied his trade on its waters, and certainly the tourist boat has replaced the fishing boat, but Marnie and I were about to embark on a trip that Jesus took, and that was good enough for us.

The Sea of Galilee is 32 miles in circumference and lies within the Great Syrian-African Rift Valley. We had now traveled completely around the lake in the last two days. The time had come to return to our cottage by the lake and what better way than to take a boat ride across the widest part of the sea from Ginosar Harbor to En GeV Harbor, a trip of just over seven miles. We would be traveling from the northwest corner of the lake towards the southeast. We would be sailing over the deepest part of the lake, depths reaching 157 feet. We had picked a calm day to make our journey though there was a slight breeze that did ripple the surface just a bit. It was easy to see just how quick the Sea of Galilee could turn into a raging ocean. The lakes in the northern tip of Maine have similar characteristics. I have been caught out on such lakes a number of times while salmon fishing with my father-in-law, Stacy Meister, and the experience is not pleasant. One minute the water is as smooth as glass, and within minutes you are fighting three foot swells all because of the change of the wind direction and speed. We had no such event on our trip, but deep down we all knew that a sudden change in the weather could stir the sea into a cauldron of fury. (Did we secretly wish it?)

As we got underway (a motorized craft) our boat was filled with not only our group but other tourists making the trek from west to east. The first thoughts that came were these verses about Jesus making a similar trip: *"And when he [Jesus] was entered into a ship, his disciples followed him. And, behold, there arose a great tempest in the sea . . ." (Matthew 8:23) "And he [Jesus] entered into a ship, and passed over, and came into his own city [Capernaum]." (Matthew 9:1)* In the instruction booklet they gave us for our classes in Israel I learned that the prevailing winds come from the west, from the Mediterranean. The strongest wind, however, comes from the Golan in the winter which was probably the case when Jesus and the disciples came up against "a great wind that blew." (John 6:18) I was told that waves as high as twelve feet have been recorded at Tiberias. For those of us who live on the ocean, those are ocean heights. We know that Jesus was familiar with maritime weather forecasting because he made mention of them when he was debating with his skeptics about the signs of the times (Matthew 16:1-4). Our Galilee "galleon" trip across the Sea of Galilee was a wonderful teaching experience.

57.

SEA SITE

Halfway across the Sea of Galilee the operator of the ship stopped the engines, and we floated in the middle of the lake for about ten minutes. We could see clearly the outcropping that was the Arbel Cliffs directly to our west. Looking more southwestward, we could see Tiberias in the late afternoon haze. To the north we couldn't make out Capernaum or Bethsaida, but we basically knew where they could be found on the shoreline and the Lower Golan Heights rose gently upward directly to our east. It was then Greg pointed out a distinctive mount directly in front of the bow about three miles away. It stood out even against the higher hill of Bashan behind it. This was the Decapolis city of Hippus, a dominate town in the region just a few miles from En GeV Resort. I had noticed its distinct cone-shaped hill when we drove into the resort, but only on our ride across the Sea of Galilee was its history revealed. Greg said that some believe that this might have been the city Jesus was referring to when he said, "A city that is set on a hill cannot be hid." (Matthew 5:14) It certainly stood out as a ruined hilltop. I couldn't imagine what it must have looked like when fully lit up at night. It was just another imagery that now fills my mind when I read Jesus' Sermon on the Mount, and, yes, you can make out Hippus on a clear day from Mount Arbel.

As I took in the sights and sites from the middle of the lake, I could understand why Josephus described the landscape around the Sea of Galilee as "the ambition of nature." The mild climate, natural beauty, and the presence of therapeutic thermal springs still make it a favorite tourist destination for health and holiday to this day. Eugene Hoade once described the lake like this: "I believe that there are more beautiful lakes in the world set in a more enchanting surrounding, but I still believe that there is not in the world a more fascinating lake. Look at its azure blue in deep sleep without a ripple on its bosom: the little sailing boats as if just painted on the canvas; not a breath of air to disturb in its waters the great reflections of the surrounding mountains. It is a joy that leads on to hour less contemplation." And contemplating I was as the engine started up, and we headed for a landing just a couple of miles north of our resort. The plan for the evening was a fish fry at a well-known eating establishment in En GeV Harbor. We were to taste Saint Peter's fish, or Mush, sometimes called Peter's perch. The lake was still extremely rich in fish, and according to Greg and Joel this restaurant was the best place to experience Galilee's favorite fish, or was it?

I was having mixed feelings about the special supper for two reasons. After you taste fresh fish from the Gulf of Maine, any other fish in the world is second rate at best, and in Maine perch is a trash fish only used for bait. Second, if we stayed for supper we would miss swimming in the Sea of Galilee. Because we got in late the night before, Marnie and I only had a few minutes to enjoy the warm water of the lake. In the end, Marnie and I decided to skip supper and swim. Of our group only one other, Ike Spiker, made the same choice. Ike is a diabetic, and he knew that he could only swim once in the Sea, and this night was that night. So after a 45-minute boat ride across the Sea of Galilee, we walked 35 minutes back to EnGev Resort to enjoy another Galilee sunset and swim. I will never regret our decision to forego a meal of Galilean perch to the pleasure we had on the beach at En Gev. Marnie, Ike, and I had the place to ourselves for nearly an hour. A few of our comrades who had supper did make it back to watch the sun set behind the Cliffs of Arbel. We talked of our day and the great sites we had seen.

58.

SEA SURGE

There is something powerful and thrilling in the sound of the surf from a troubled sea against a stony coast. The roar is so loud that I have stood on the coast of Maine many times unable to hear my companion speak to me by my side. I believe the first time I heard that soul-touching noise was on my honeymoon in the beginning of the summer of 1973.

My bride and I had made a part of our honeymoon a trip to Bar Harbor, a traditional Maine honeymoon. Because both of us had been landlocked in northern Maine for the bulk of our lives, we didn't know what to expect when we crossed from the mainland in Trenton to Mount Desert Island. Our travels around the island took us through some very scenic places like Seal Cove and Otter Creek. It was love at first sight because the sites were beyond our imagination. Little did we know we had a seashore streak in our DNA, and little did we know that we would be spending the bulk of our ministry life off or on the coastline of Maine (at the time of this writing 31 years)? We drove up Cadillac Mountain, but the fog was so thick that we could hardly see each other. It would be many, many years (1973-1991) later when we moved officially to Ellsworth that we would see for the first time the marvelous, magnificent sights from that seaside knoll that people travel hundreds and sometimes thousands of miles to see. Not discouraged, we drove off the hill (after you have scaled mountains, you soon learn what the locals call a mountain is in reality just a hill) and headed around the

Park (Acadia National Park) Loop Road. We passed Great Head and Sand Beach, but stopped when we saw a sign that read "Thunder Hole."

The morning fog was still thick, but not thick enough at the water's edge to block out the sound of the surf. As we strolled down the pathway leading to Thunder Hole the tide was high and the wind was strong. The combination of the rising sea and the driving wind made for some spectacular surges of water up the gap between two massive granite ridges. The sound of the surge was overpowering at first. I tried to talk to my wife, but unless I spoke directly into her ear she could not hear me. It was the first time I experienced such loudness, such force of sea and stone. I have been back many times to Thunder Hole and have found the sound is not always there. I was there just last summer taking a few friends from India on a tour and Thunder Hole was barely a whisper. Years later as I reflect on that first encounter with the sound of surging surf, I thought of a similar sound that took place on Pentecost (Acts 2:2), those overwhelming impulses that sweep over our being when we are totally in tune with our resident Guest. Isaiah speaks of such a noise: "Woe to the multitude of many people, which make a noise like the noise of the seas; and to the rushing of nations, that make a rushing like the rushing of many waters." (Isaiah 17:12) Isn't it sad with such power to move and motivate others, the average Christian doesn't take advantage of the potential we have to touch others, just like that day the sea surge of Thunder Hole moved my wife and I. As the power of the sea created the tourist attraction we call Thunder Hole, so too the power of the Holy Spirit can create in us a sound that will be overpowering to the world. Yes, a sound that could turn "... *the world upside down* ..." (Acts 17:6) as our early brethren did.

The surging Spirit will come in and carry away all our sins, transgressions, and iniquities, and will leave behind Himself to lead us and direct us into all good works. That same force will shape us and break us until we are a messenger of the voice of God, just like Thunder Hole is the voice of the Atlantic Ocean on the coast of Maine.

59.

TIDE'S TIME

I still remember the first time my brother-in-Christ Calvin Greenlaw told me, "We have got to wait for the tide!" I was a new resident on Moose Island, and I knew nothing about the rising and falling of the tides in Passamaquoddy Bay especially when it came to fishing. All I knew I wanted to go fishing and I had never had to wait before. It was then I got my first lesson in the timing of the tides.

Calvin was one of the deacons of the Washington Street Baptist Church in Eastport, Maine, where I had come with my family to minister in the summer of 1986. Until then, I had never, ever looked at a tide chart as there is little need of them in the hills and hollows of northern Maine. The closest ocean spot was over two hundred miles from Westfield in Aroostook County and even further away from my hometown of Perham. Rarely did an ocean storm affect us that far away so for most of my life I didn't think much, if any, of the tides. But now I was living on an island off the coast of Maine, and the tides began to affect every aspect of my life, especially when I wanted to go flounder fishing off Campobello Island. Calvin had a friend (Ted Atsalis) who had a nice fishing boat. Ted, like me, was "from away," but had come to Eastport in the summer for years, and he had learned it was best to follow the tides because they were in charge when it came to fishing.

On our first expedition together into the bay I learned how important it was and how critical it was just to get Ted's boat in the water. Unlike most fishermen who tied up to the Eastport docks, Ted was just a seasonal visitor with no docking privileges, and, when the tide was out, it was impossible to get a boat out to sea. The more I experienced the limitations the tides forced on the resident of this small coastal community, the more I began to understand why these Mainers were so patient. They are the most patient people I have met anywhere in my life, people who had learned by living and working and resting by the seashore that one must adapt to the tides or be engulfed by them. Solomon's practical principle in Ecclesiastes is just as applicable to life on an island in Passamaquoddy Bay as it is in any aspect of life: "To everything there is a season, and a time to every purpose under heaven." (Ecclesiastes 3:1) Tide seasons and the tide's time is in God's hands as is every other "time" in Life. I know Solomon doesn't mention the tides in his listing (Ecclesiastes 3:2-7), but he could have written ". . . a time for high tide and a time for low tide . . . ," ". . . a time to go fishing and a time to refrain from fishing . . ."

How often I have resisted the tides of my life. I have tried to sail against an ebb tide only to find myself stuck in the mud of an empty cove. Instead of waiting for the flood tide of God's will, I tried and failed to make any progress in my timing. As for fishing for the souls of men (Luke 5:10), that is when your timing has to be right on. As I have learned in the tides of life, I saw demonstrated in the tides off Eastport. If you wait on the tides and work with the tides, life actually becomes quite pleasurable and plenteous, and I am not just talking about fishing. I never once went to sea with Calvin Greenlaw and Ted Atsalis on the right tide and came back empty of fish or fun; I learned to trust Calvin's understandings of the Passamaquoddy Bay tides! Why is it we have so much trouble trusting our Guide's timing? Why is it we have so much trouble waiting on our Guide's time? Why is it we have so much trouble relying on our Guide's times? As He controls the ebb and flow of the coastal tides, so too does He control the ups and downs of our lives, the stays and delays, as well as the forwards and onwards. He has given us His time chart in the Bible, and it teaches us that patience and trust is all we need to believe.

60.

DOWNDRAFT DISASTER

I walked up Casperson Beach in Florida in search of a fisherman. I couldn't imagine coming to such a body of water like the Gulf of Mexico and not do something in connection with fishing, even if it were just to watch someone fish. I have been an avid fisherman since the early 1970s with nearly 920 days on the water and over 10,000 fish to my credit, but on that wintry day in the Sunshine State I was just looking for anyone trying their luck, casting a line, and wetting some bait.

I didn't go far before up ahead was a man with two surf-casting rods in the sand. Despite the fact he was the only fisherman in sight, I thought at least one man wasn't letting all this water go to waste. However, as I neared his fishing hole my attention was drawn away to the many birds that were also gathering on the rocks jutting out from the beach at that point along the shore. Such obstacles are always a good place to fish because the rock formations are protection for smaller fish, and where there are small fish there are larger fish wanting a meal. At first I thought the birds might be waiting for the fisherman's success, but soon I realized that it was something more.

Next to fishing, I love watching birds in flight, or any creature in nature, especially the wild ones. I marvel at the God-given ability of birds, living on the edge of the wind, to soar and glide and fly above the earth or sea in the firmament. During my days in Florida I watched the terns and seagulls as I often do on the coast of Maine. I live twenty miles from the actual Gulf of Maine, but the seagulls are a common fixture in our city of Ellsworth. When I try to feed the local raven colony, the seagulls unusually beat the raven to the meal. What I liked best in Florida was my first up close and personal encounter with pelicans. There are no such creatures on Maine's shore. What an ugly bird I first thought, certainly nothing like our majestic Maine bald eagle, and certainly not in the same class as the crow or the osprey of Maine. As I drew near to the fishermen and the pelicans sitting on the rocky breakwater, both seemed unconcerned with my approach. "A real ugly bird," I thought again as I asked the fisherman if he had any success.

They don't even seem to like flying I thought as the fisherman reported to me that he had caught nothing all morning. My attention turned from the unsuccessful fisherman and the uninterested pelicans to the seagulls and the terns drifting effortlessly along the updrafts created by the sea and the shore. "Probably so heavy they can't get off the rocks," I thought as I couldn't keep my eye off the pelicans; they kept drawing me back. Then I thought back to my scriptures and how God listed the pelican among the "dirty [unclean] birds" (Leviticus 11:18 and Deuteronomy 14:17). I also recalled this from the Psalmist: ". . . I am like a pelican in the wilderness . . ." (Psalm 102:6) Despite their ugly, awkward appearance, I thought how wise they were in waiting until there was enough wind to carry them aloft. Wise is the bird who knows how to adjust to the wind. We humans insist on testing the winds of fortune and misfortune instead of waiting for a favorable wind. We test fate in our arrogance, pride, and haughtiness only to encounter the cross winds of calamity. We try to soar against the downdrafts of disaster and more often than not crash and burn. We try sailing against the wind shear of worry and set our flight and fly right into fret and fear. As I watched the pelicans on Casperson Beach, I began to realize that their strength was in knowing when to soar and when to set. I remembered, "The fowl of the air . . . O Lord our God, how excellent is they name in all the earth." (Psalm 8:8-9) Instead of bucking a contrary gale, we need to learn to wait a fine breeze.

61.

FULL FLOOD

Years ago I put together a collection of remembrances under the caption of "My Maine Memory." The last one in this series dealt with a memory I recalled from a phrase from the Book of Job: "... *He maketh the sea like a pot of ointment.*" (Job 41:31) In this article I would like to share with my reader what this Biblical phrase meant to me.

Living in northern Maine for nearly half my life, I had the opportunity to witness the Aurora Borealis many times. Those luminous bands of colorful lights in the night sky have always impressed me each and every time I have had the privilege of watching God's laser show. If I had never moved to the coast of Maine, probably they would go down as the most awesome sights I have seen in the nature of Maine.

Rainbows have also been a fascination to me over the years in Maine. Recently, I witnessed a perfect double rainbow. The colors were brilliant and bright, and they were highlighted by a deep blue sky, simply awesome, but again if I hadn't moved to the seaside of Downeast Maine these rainbows or the Aurora Borealis would be the finest displays of nature in my native state. But when I saw the tides of Eastport, my mind was changed. There is something extraordinary about watching a full flood in bays and coves.

I came to Eastport at a low tide in my life. I had just finished my second difficult ministry. Twelve years of nearly empty service. Oh, there had been the occasional high tide, but very soon the bays and coves of my life were empty again through the critical spirits that surrounded me. As I drove across the causeway from Pleasant Point (the Passamaquoddy Indian Reservation) to Quoddy Village (the town that was built during the quest to harness the Passamaquoddy tides), the tide was almost out. Mud flats and rocky shoals were about all you could see, but very little water. Far away, far offshore I could see just a bit of sea, but it seemed so far away, too far away to affect my life I thought. So much of my spiritual life in the service of the King had resulted in a spiritual emptiness, a spiritual void. Was Eastport going to be just another ebb tide experience? Where would my balm of Gilead (Jeremiah 8:22) come from on Moose Island?

As we moved into the parsonage on the only road coming into the village of Eastport, the tide in Passamaquoddy Bay began to switch. I stood in amazement at the volume of sea water that surged into the empty coves and corners surrounding the small island. I was experiencing my first natural high tide. The full weight of the Atlantic Ocean changed everything around Moose Island. The ugly clam flats were gone as were the seaweed-covered rocks, gone! The coastline had changed from a smelly eyesore to a beautiful haven highlighted by rugged seashore and underlined by granite walls carpeted by green trees and greener grass (we arrived in August). At full flood tide the Maine Island turned into an emerald in the middle of a bright, blue sea.

What took place in the bay that afternoon also took place in my heart. Over the next five years at the Washington Street Baptist Church, I experienced what it felt like to have a full flood tide encounter with Christians and the Church. How different the time in Eastport was compared to my other two churches. What happened there would continue when I moved down the coast to Ellsworth, an overflowing, overwhelming, all-engulfing kindness and love of God's people, and a full, flood tide of God's goodness and graciousness. I discovered a people that accepted me for who I was and what I was. Their support, like the high tide, was uplifting, enfolding, and their surge of caring for me and my family was so encouraging— just how it ought to be in the brotherhood of Christ.

62.

SEA SAND

How many times does the Bible speak of "the sand of the sea?" Often it is used in the numbering of Israel (Genesis 22:17), the amount of corn Joseph gathered (Genesis 41:49), the Canaanite army that came against Joshua (Joshua 11:4), or the numbering of the nations (Revelation 20:8), but for me this phrase has another meaning.

Whether walking along a beach in Maine or in Florida, in California or in Israel, in Alaska or in India, the sand seems to be the same to me; whether I am strolling along the sandy shores of New Jersey, the sand seems the same to me. Whether I am plodding the shoreline or Kerala or Australia, the sand seems the same to me. It is because, you see, I know nothing about sand. The sand of one beach must be a bit different than the sand of another beach in size, texture, or color, but to me it is all sand. I know I have experienced other materials mixed in with the sand like broken seashells, shark's teeth, fragments of concrete, pieces of wood, sea glass, and other scattered material washed in on the tide. But despite these foreign items mingled among the grains of sand, the beach is always more sand than any other material. You might find a pebble here or there, even a good size rock, but nothing is greater in volume than the sand itself, those tiny, fine stones we call sand.

What is it about sand that we love? Is it the way it feels when we walk barefoot on it? Can it be the sensation that comes when the sand gets between our toes and sooths our weary feet? Is it the sheer mass of it stretching on for miles along the coastline of Florida or just a few feet in the tiny cove that we find along the rugged shoreline of Maine? For a few it is building sand castles. Just yesterday I was watching the local news, and they had the story of a man that has been constructing sand castles for most of his life. An engineer, he makes elaborate structures on the beach near his home that amazes the beachcombers that witness his works of art. Asked why he spends so much time on something that will last but a few hours, and his reply is "I just love sand." Whatever it is, people have been flocking to sandy beaches for centuries for the love of sand.

For me sand contains another parable of spiritual truth most humans have missed. Isaiah 10:22 says, "For though thy people Israel be as the sand of the sea, yet a remnant of them shall return . . ." Imagine with me that each sand granular is a person, a human being. We forget that God sees us this way. To Him we are as small as one tiny pebble on the seashore. Mankind has forgotten just how big God is and how small we are. Isaiah speaks of the earth as God's footstool (Isaiah 66:1), and if the entire world is a place for God's feet then mankind is like the sand of the seashore between His toes! For me mankind is moving toward a full arrogance and diluted haughtiness in thinking he is big and powerful and significant in the world he lives in. In reality he is but a grain of sand packed together in his cities like the sand on a beach building his sand castles which will be washed away on the rise of the judgment tide of God. Some of the great ancient cities like Babylon are now just a pile of sand, and where are the people? They are gone. Just a few months ago I made my first visit to Long Beach Island off the coast of New Jersey. While there I talked to a local resident about Hurricane Sandy and what it did to the beaches along the twenty-two mile long shore. I was shocked when he said that all the sand that I was now walking on was new sand because the beach sand had been replaced after Sandy. Then I thought how the pride of man in his billions thinks he can sustain a divine onslaught worse than a hurricane, but he can't and won't because of Revelation 6:8 (read it yourself)! Billions will be swept away in a divine judgment like the sand of the sea being washed away in a hurricane.

63.

SANDY SHORE

"A stone is heavy, and the sand weighty; but a fool's wrath is heavier than them both." (Proverbs 27:3) Do you see the sermonette from the seashore in this Solomonic statute?

Have you ever filled a bucket with sand? Despite being small in size, a grain of sand multiplies in weight with each grain of sand added to your collection, and the density of the combined granules only adds in weight as the volume of sand increases. That is why wet sand makes such good building material for sand castles, and why I like the analogy Solomon makes in his proverb printed above. Men without God (fools says Psalm 14:1) build their sand castles on the shores of time, and mankind continues to build his cities on the sandy shores of history. Like the first Babylonians (Genesis 11), they built their first sand castle (a tower), and their children have been following their example ever since. As the sand of a seashore sticks together so too was the dream of the Babylonians to stay together (Genesis 11:4) despite the fact God had commanded them to disperse (Genesis 9:1). What fools they were thinking God wouldn't notice (Genesis 11:5). But He did and in the end confused them by giving them different languages. What I have found amazing is that the world's nations are still trying to return to their one beach.

Even to this day there is a movement to join the world again into one United Nation, one economic system, one religious worship, and one beach of sandy sand; weighty, powerful, and united against what? In one of the great prophetic psalms David tells us of the final goal of this collection of sand: "Why do the heathen rage and the people imagine a vain thing? The kings of the earth set themselves, and the rulers take counsel together, against the Lord, and against His anointed [Jesus], saying, let us break their bands asunder, and cast away their cords from us." (Psalm 2:1-3) The sand is saying to its Maker that it doesn't want any more control on it. The leaders of the world's sand will one day rebel against the Almighty and His Son Jesus Christ. The folly of this is like the sand on a sandy shore saying it wants to control the sea; it wants to be in charge. Oh, the sand is weighty and numerous, but on any given day there is no doubt in the mind of the beachcomber who is in charge—the sea. It is the sea that shapes the beach and molds the beach in its own image not the other way around. And so it is with God and mankind.

Mankind dreams its little dreams of what it will do even against its Creator. They dig their deep moats around their superior sand castles built in the ambitions and aspirations of being safe, self-protected, and secure behind the walls of their own creation. They shape their plans, self-interest, and self-gratification into their sand structures thinking they are in control of the future, their time, and destiny. But like with the sand castle village I watched my daughter Marnie and our Indian driver Binu make on Eve's Beach in Kovalam, Kerala in 2007, eventually the entire creation was washed away in the rising tide of the Arabian Sea. So too shall the plans of man to resist the onslaught of the armies of heaven, like a rising tide, will sweep them all away (Revelation 19:11-21). That is way God laughs (Psalm 2:4) at their folly, their foolish dreams, and the fools that they are. Their wrath against the Almighty is certainly heavier than the weighty sand, but just as incompetent as the sandy shore to resist the power and might of the sea.

I like the way Phillip Keller put it in his book Sea Edge: *"Yes, not only do we plan and build and scheme and work to erect our sand castles, we also forget that the tides of time and the power of God's presence are as inexorable as the ocean tides rising in response to the gravitational pull of the moon!"* Ultimately, God will have the last laugh.

64.

REFRESHING REEF

It was after I started visiting the seashore and seaside places that I learned this little chorus from my wife: *"Times of refreshing here in Your Presence, no greater blessing than being with you. My soul is restored, my mind is renewed; there is no greater joy Lord than being with you!"* And it was while I was visiting a small Christian campground in Weston, Maine, that I found the verse that verifies the meaning of the tiny chorus: *"Repent ye therefore, and be converted, that your sins may be blotted out, when the times of refreshing shall come from the presence of the Lord."* (Acts 3:19) I was in between my daily morning and evening sessions with the kids trying to persuade them into being converted when I thought again of my times of refreshing with the Lord while walking and strolling by the refreshing reefs of my life.

What I love best about Christian camping and walks along the sea edge is the solitude. Living Waters Bible Camp is situated on the shores of East Grand Lake, and while it isn't the ocean or a sea, it could be called an inland sea because of its size which is large enough to be partly in Maine and the rest of it in the Canadian province of New Brunswick. Despite being with seventy kids and fifty staffers, the size of the camp and the vastness of the lake make you feel that you're alone, just like those times you walk alone along some distance beach. Instead of being mesmerized by things and stuff, the kids get a chance to come aside and spend some time with God. Instead of being bombarded by a thousand false voices calling them to do a thousand things aside from God, they at least have a chance to hear "the still small voice" calling them to Himself. Instead of being assaulted by the perverted propaganda which only calls them to leisure, pleasure, or some kind of treasure that will fade or rust, they get a chance to learn about things that have eternal value. God created man, even kids, for stillness and quietness, and it has been for me a coveted quest to find those refreshing reefs.

Whether my first reef on Australia's southern shore or Kerala's reef on Eve's Beach, I have treasured my solitude times on the ocean's edge as the waters wash back and forth over those rocky reefs. It was in such place I discovered a divine serenity, a godly solitude that became a balm for my brain and a solace for my soul, just like the lawns and fields of Living Waters Camp, a small fragment of this earth that is still in pristine shape. Some might be distracted by the cabins, chapels, and cottages scattered around, but the bit of beach that highlights one of hundreds of coves on East Grand Lake soon brings you back to a sense of stillness and a marvellous silence. Interestingly, a small reef is located just off shore, a ridge underwater that attracts smallmouth bass. Just last night after chapel while the kids were playing "a game of finding the counselor," I stood on the dock where the boat that pulls the "banana" (you don't want to know) and the party boat that takes the kids fishing (another responsibility I have at camp) are tied. Oh, I could hear the howling and hooting behind me, but when I turned my back and focused my cast to the reef before me, I was lost in the solitude and serenity.

It was nearly nine and the half moon was shining bright. A few mosquitos were out and a few bass were biting, but none of this was as refreshing as the cool night air and being alone with God. Many are afraid of being alone at night in a wooded area by a lake, but for me it was just another example of a time of refreshing by a reef in the presence of the Maker of the lake, the reef, and the bass. When will we learn that God's first desire after the creation of man was to walk with him ". . . in the cool of the day . . ." (Genesis 3:8)

65.

WAVE-WASHED

If I were asked to name only one sound that I love to listen to on the seashore, I would have a hard time. I enjoy the myriad of sounds that are found near the water's edge. Think with me. There is the sound of the seabirds as they look for their next lunch. There are the varying sounds of the wind depending on the force of the breeze or the gust of the gale. There is the sound of the surf, or the sound of the breakers off shore, or the sound of the sea crashing into some breakwater or pile of rocks. I have heard them all and enjoy them all, but if I were asked only to name one sea sound, what would that sound be? I think for me it would be the gentle sound of a wave washing a bit of beach. Not a roaring wave, but that little wave that comes in when the sea is calm. Do you know the sound I'm speaking of? If you are any beachcomber at all you know that sound.

The Psalmist more often than not writes of a boisterous wave like he does in Psalm 93:4: "The Lord on high is mightier than the noise of many waters, yea, than the mighty waves of the sea." And certainly God can seem that way, the way He was on Mount Sinai when out of a great thunder cloud He spoke to the children of Israel (Exodus 19-20). Granted, at times the ocean proclaims such a voice, but most of the time it is more like "the still small voice" that Elijah heard on that very same mountain (I Kings 19:8-12). A weak whisper, a still sound, audible but barely heard. Sometimes on the beaches where I find such a low sound I am distracted by the beach goers, the birds above, or the noise of civilization near the water's edge.

Even in the pristine places there are distractors, but if your quest is to find that sound then you must get close to the shore, find a solitude place, and listen. If you are looking for quiet communion with the waves washing the shore then you must be still yourself. You must set your mind on pause, you must tune your heart to waves, and you must still your soul until all you hear and feel are the waves lapping at your feet. It will be then you will find your connection and will not be disappointed with the time you spend with the wave-washed beach.

If you are also looking for a quiet time with your Maker then this is the time, a time to be still (Psalm 46:10) and know that He is there with you. Just a few short months ago (four to be exact), I was searching for such a place on Long Beach Island off the Jersey Shore. I was there to grieve and mourn the departure of my 39-year old son. I left my coastline city of Ellsworth, Maine, for this deserted shoreline (only in April) to get away from the telephone calls (calling to tell me how sorry they were at Scott's passing), doorbells (people coming by to pay their respects and regrets), and mail delivery (countless sympathy cards and letter). What I desire most in times of sorrow is solitude; what I desire most in times of sadness is stillness; what I desire most in times of tragedy is time alone with God. I found it all on the 22-mile long beach on a barrier island off the coastline of New Jersey. Peace pervaded the place because it wasn't tourist season. Calm caressed my soul as I stepped out on my first long walk up the shoreline. The song that the surf was singing filled the air, and a sublime sense of the Spirit of God was there.

I walked and talked with the Almighty, and the gulls didn't seem to mind our conversation. It was there on that wave-washed shore I heard "the still small voice" of God, and we settled once and for all why he took Scott (between me and Him). As that gentle sound rolled in from the sea, the gentle voice of God calmed my soul and refreshed my spirit so I knew I could go on, return to Ellsworth to minister, and to take up again my responsibly because of a wave-washed encounter with my Lord.

66.

SEASIDE SERMONETTE

Moses had taught Israel centuries before: "Hear, O Israel: the Lord our God is one Lord." (Deuteronomy 6:4) David spoke of the Holy One in his prophecy about the Christ's death (Psalm 16:10). Despite the confusion this concept has generated over the years, belief in this doctrine is a fundamental cornerstone in our Christian Faith. Dennis DeHaan writing in an Our Daily Bread article gives us these challenging words about this theology, and I quote, "The idea of the One God in three Persons has long been baffling to the human mind. But to reject it has given rise to cults and many false teachings. The problem is not the doctrine itself but our inability to understand it. It is said that Saint Augustine, the famous early church theologian, was walking on the shore of the ocean one day pondering the mystery of the trinity. He came upon a little boy who was playing with a seashell. The youngster would scoop a hole in the sand, then go down to the waves and get his shell full of water and pour it into the hole he had made. Augustine said, 'what are you doing, my little fellow?' The boy replied: 'I am going to pour the sea into that hole!' 'Ah,' said Augustine, 'that is what I am trying to do. Standing at the ocean of infinity, I have attempted to grasp it with my finite mind.' The trinity does not fit the framework of common logic, nor can it be fully analyzed by the microscope of man's intellect. But this is no reason to say it is the invention of theologians. To declare that the One and only God has made Himself known as Father, Son, and Holy Spirit—three distinct, not separate, persons—is simply an attempt to define what the Scriptures teach. (John 10:29-30 and Acts 5:3-4) But to commit our lives to this triune God is to begin to see with the eye of faith His greatness as our Creator, Redeemer, and Sustainer. And doesn't it make sense that the "One" we worship, and to whom we entrust our lives, should be vastly greater than our limited ability to understand Him? Father, Son, and Holy Spirit, O thou blessed trinity: One in essence yet three Persons, thou art God, and we worship Thee. The idea of a triune God staggers the mind, but to know Him satisfies the heart!"

Remember, what Jesus said according to John 10:20: "I and my Father are One." And then there is what Paul wrote to the young man Timothy, "Now unto the King eternal, immortal, invisible, the only wise God, be honour and glory forever and ever, Amen!" (I Timothy 1:17) My attention was drawn to this verse, seeing I learned this verse in a chorus when I was just a lad, because of the desire of some in this world to unite all the "gods" because a multitude of "gods" is so much better than the belief of a single, triune God. This isn't a new philosophy in the world, but this is certainly a new belief in the United States of America where Christianity has been the dominate faith since our beginning. Christian America is how I have always seen our land, but years ago on a visit to Washington D. C. I came face to face with the changing America. As I walked through the National Cathedral I met a tour guide and asked, "What denomination is this church?" He replied, "Episcopal, but all faiths worship here, and all 'gods' are honored here." I was shocked. I was surprised. I was stunned. I didn't know my nation had slipped into the worship of all gods, and that no longer was One God a part of our national religion. As my family and I walked around Washington D. C., we saw churches, chapels, and cathedrals to all the known and unknown gods of many nations. By the time our tour was over I felt like climbing the steps to the Capital building and shout at the top of my lungs, "Hear, O America: the Lord our God is one Lord." But I am afraid it would be as successful as standing on the ocean's edge and yelling, "Be Gone!.

67.

SEASCAPE SHAPING

The most spectacular seascape I know use to be owned by a dear friend of mine from Moose Island, an island off the downeast coast of Maine. At the time of this "sermonette from the seashore" my friend has just turned 90, and his family is in the church as I am typing my notes in preparation of a surprise birthday party for him. A modest bungalow owned by Calvin and Annalie set high on a bluff overlooking Passamaquoddy Bay. (The Greenlaws sold their bayside house a few years ago and moved to Ellsworth where their only grandchildren live.) While ministering in Eastport, I had the privilege of visiting that seaside home countless times. Below the bluff was a stretch of beach I loved to walk at low tide. Whether standing on the ocean side cliff or strolling in its shadow, I learned a lot about this Biblical precept from the Psalmist David: "Many are the afflictions of the righteous: but the Lord delivereth him out of them all." (Psalm 34:19)

Many were the afflictions of Greenlaw bluff, Greenlaw bungalow, and Greenlaw beach. I have watched the pounding of a surging surf and the crashing of huge waves day after day after day in an onslaught that should have destroyed that section of the Maine coastline. I have witnessed gale force winds combined with winter rain that should have washed the Greenlaw house into the sea. I have wondered why thousands upon thousands of seasonal storms off Campobello Island over the centuries haven't dissolved away that bluff and melted that cliff into the ocean. Yet, the combined storms haven't, and what is true of that seascape is true of the saint.

I learned in my five years on Moose Island that it was the sea and surf, the wind and the waves, the tides and the times that had shaped and sculpted the character of the cliffs overlooking Greenlaw Beach. But instead of seeing the ugly scars of savage storms or the shattered stones of titanic tides, I saw beauty in the rugged face of the bluff. The seascape that I have come to admire was the result of heavy seas, driving winds, and rising tides. We might see those results as affliction against the land, but it was in their shaping that the landscape was fashioned. We know the finished product as I saw it is not finished, but an ongoing process, an evolution of an ever-changing seascape, and so it is in the life of every saint. Affliction is not for annihilation, it is for an effect. Trouble isn't for termination, it is for testing. Difficulty isn't for destruction, it is for development. As the good Lord through His nature shapes and molds the Maine seascape on Moose Island, He shapes us into the image of His precious Son Jesus through affliction. (Romans 8:29)

Why is Greenlaw beach, Greenlaw bluff, and that old battered Greenlaw bungalow an iconic picture, a painting worth painting, a landscape worth buying? For me the answer is a simple one: because I know they have endured all severe storms, all fierce winds, and every gale and gust, and they still stand today waiting the next storm, gale, or rain. The very nature of man is to avoid the difficult, the dangerous, and the destructive. Yet it is at such times, during these abrasive and abusive actions our character is shaped, our integrity is sculptured, and our morals are molded. Jesus was very clear that we would face tribulations (John 16:31), but as He overcame His so would we overcome ours and be made into His glorious character. Tests, trials, and tribulations are the tools the Master sculptor uses to shape our soulscape. Mysteriously, the very things that would seemingly destroy us will instead strengthen us. Wondrously, the very things that afflict us actually benefit us. Incredibly, the very things that harm us will help us to be more like Him. Soulscaping is a lot like seascaping; God uses afflictions to sculpture both.

68.

SAND SERMON

It was the great Hebrew prophet Jeremiah that penned these Words of the Almighty: "Fear ye not me? saith the Lord: will ye not tremble at my presence, which have placed the sand for the bound of the sea by perpetual decree, that it cannot pass it: and though the waves thereof toss themselves, yet can they not prevail; though they roar, yet can they not pass over it?" (Jeremiah 5:22) I probably would have never understood that verse if I hadn't at times visited the seaside and witnessed for myself the constant struggle between sea and sand.

I don't know if Jeremiah ever actually watched this titanic wrestling match between sand and surf, but he certainly could have seeing he lived less than 26 miles from the Mediterranean Sea. It doesn't matter whether or not Jeremiah walked the seacoast of Israel because he wrote under inspiration (II Peter 1:21) and was inspired to write these lines. Because we believe that all Scripture is given by inspiration and is profitable (II Timothy 3:16), there is a sand sermon here for us to listen too. What Jeremiah wrote happens every moment of every day on a sea shore. No barriers can be seen between a stretch of beach sand and the mighty sea except when man tries to construct one. It appears at first to the amateur beachcomber a David against Goliath conflict. At first glance it appears that the sand can't win because of miles and miles of deep oceans versus comparably a few feet of sand. As the strength of the tide increases and the waves enlarge, it seems as if the weight and volume of water would soon swallow the narrow strip of sand. As I have walked the beaches around the world, I witnessed again and again the rise and crashing of the waves against the beach. In some places I have watched as the water does overwhelm the sand, and the water reaches its mighty hands to the tender grassline, the stately treeline, or the rocky shoreline. It seems the sand will be washed away, carried away into the ocean deep, but at the turning of the tide the sand always settles back to its original place, and at low tide the victory has been won. It is kind of like the old fable about the tortoise and the hare. The hare ought to win, but always loses to the tortoise, and so it is with the sea and the sand. Solomon speaks of "... the sand weighty ..." (Proverbs 27:3), and no matter how many times the ocean sweeps over the sand, the sand will remain. No matter how hard the ocean tries to carry the sand away, it can't, but why? Jeremiah has given us the answer to this riddle of nature.

We know from Jeremiah's quoting the Almighty that on the beach, in the battle between sand and sea, there is another force at work, an invisible force no man can actual see. Like the wind you can see the effect, but not the actual wind. The Creator and Maker and Designer (remember, the triune God was totally involved in the creation) of the seas have determined that the sand will be the barrier of the sea. No matter how much the ocean may roar at its forced limitations, it still can only go so far up the shore. The sand will be its restrainer. This sermon has been written in the sand for all to see. The tragedy is few stop long enough in their day by the sea to hear or see this sermon. I will probably never fully comprehend all the sermonettes by the sea, but I now have heard this sermon. God does make limits. Whether the sea or Satan, each can only go so far (read Job 1-2). Remember the great test God allowed Satan to make on God's man in Uz? At first Satan could touch Job's stuff, but could go no further. Then Satan could touch Job's health, but could not take his life. How Satan roared at such restrictions, but no matter the protest, he could only go so far, just like the sea. And this sermon is for us.

69.

BEACH BREEZE

Recently, I had to return to my old ministry town of Eastport for the funeral of a former parishioner that I had promised nine years before to attend her departure (II Timothy 4:6). When I left my home in Ellsworth the temperature was in the upper 40s and the forecast told of 50s, a very nice temperature for the early part of March in Maine. I had dressed for summer having forgotten how cold the breeze off Passamaquoddy Bay could be in March. When I got out of my car to talk to Jim Spinney (a former deacon of mine at the Washington Street Baptist Church) at his garage, I immediately felt a frost crawling up my neck. Despite the cold reception, I was reminded in my afternoon's return to the sea that beach breezes do breathe their own form of praise: "Let everything that hath breath praise the Lord. Praise ye the Lord." (Psalm 150:6)

My second stop before the funeral was at another deacon's (Calvin Greenlaw) home overlooking the bay. Calvin's house sets high on a bluff overlooking the Canadian island of Campobello about three miles away. It was breezy on Washington Street where Jim's garage was located (actually right across the street from the church sanctuary), but the wind was blowing a gale at Calvin's place. I had been there often when I pastored the church in the late 1980s, and I knew about the ocean breezes, but on that morning I think I had forgotten a few things about a beach breeze. The first thing I remembered was how much I enjoyed them, cold or warm. I had learned early on in my stay on Moose Island that the seashore doesn't write the songs played on the bluffs, the breeze does. The beach doesn't shape the sounds, the wind does. The beach and the bluffs are but amplifiers of the zephyr that blows around that bend in the shoreline. It was there along that strand of sand that I learned that if you listen carefully "everything that hath breathe does praise the Lord," and I learned on Greenlaw Bluff that the breeze does have a breathe.

I had been away long enough to have forgotten how nice it is to breathe deeply two lungs of sea breeze even if the sea breeze was Arctic cold. There is something just plain invigorating about a beach breeze in March. Maybe it has to do with the strength and power of the ocean that drives it or the salty taste the sea provides. Maybe it is the combination of the wind and the waves that is vital to the refreshing of one's body as well as one's soul. All I know is that there is something special about a sea breeze that reassures the observer that God's creation is praising Him even when His crowning design isn't. Fresh Praise! Inexhaustible Praise! And fresh adoration with every breeze, with every breath of the sea. Few of us take time to listen, but God does. Isaiah tells us that in heaven there are a group of angels that do nothing but praise the Lord night and day unendingly (Isaiah 6:2-3). I have come to believe that choir on earth are the breezes of the beach. Standing on a coastal bluff brings one to a meeting of great forces and those forces are all breathing the same thing, "Praise ye the Lord! Praise ye the Lord!"

I left Eastport after Gladys Logan's funeral, but not before I drove Calvin back to his end of the island. (We actually buried Gladys in a cemetery located at the tip of Moose Island that overlooks Passamaquoddy Bay, and the breeze was there in all its might and glory praising the homegoing of a great saint of God.) I couldn't help but stop for one more look as I turned the corner below his home before heading out of town. I couldn't help rolling down my car window and take in one more salty breath before heading home. The wind was still howling and the breeze was still frosty, but the message to me was clear. The sermonette from the seashore was heard saying, "Let everything that hath breath . . .

70.

SAND SCULPTURES

Who of us hasn't built a sand castle, or some kind of sand sculpture, and watched as the incoming tide washed it away? All our hard work and inspired imagination, gone in a few rolls of the sea; all our energy, all our effort, swept away as the sea reclaims its treasured sand and deposits it back on the beach smooth and refreshed as if it never knew the shape we had created.

I have recently finished reading a marvellous devotional book by Phillip Keller entitled "Songs of the Soul" in which he makes this application to sand castles and sand sculptures. I quote: "All of us build our sand castles on the sands of time. All of us dream our little dreams of what we shall do with our lives. We dig our deep moats around those very private ambitions. We carefully erect our walls of self-protection to surround our elaborate aspirations. We shape and mold our decisions and personal choices into castles of self-interest and self-gratification. Most of us do this happily, blithely in our youth. We behave as though there were only time, lots of time, and us. There seem to be so many years ahead, so many seasons to carry out our schemes, so many days to do our thing. We forget so soon that God is even there; and though He is, He seems as remote as the moon that turns the beach to silver at night. Yes, not only do we plan and build and scheme and work to erect our sand castles, we also forget that the tides of time and the power of God's presence are as inexorable as the ocean tides rising in response to the gravitational pull of the moon. For in the full flood of high tide under the rising surge of the incoming wave, beneath the sweeping course of the ocean currents, the castle, the walls, the moats, the work of our dreams will disappear, lost in oblivion. Such is the end of those aims and ambitions built in thoughtless, careless abandon without reckoning on the power of God. Beautiful but for a day, they are swept away into nothing. Lord, help me to build on the Rock!"

What Keller was writing about is what Jesus once spoke about: "Therefore whosoever heareth these sayings of mine, and doeth them, I will liken him unto a wise man, which built his house upon a rock . . . And every one that heareth these sayings of mine, and doeth them not, shall be likened unto a foolish man which built his house upon the sand: and the rain descended, and the floods came, and the winds blew, and beat upon the house; and it fell: and great was the fall of it." (Matthew 7:24, 26, 27) So many of us think that our sand castle, our sand sculpture can be solved by a sea wall. I have watched as the sand castle nears completion a second construction project begins. Many try to shield their sand castles by building elaborate barriers, sea walls of insurance, barriers of health management, and defenses of lifestyle changes. We try everything to guard our dreams, our plans, and our assets only in time to see our castle crumble and our sculpture vanish because our sea wall has proven, as they all do, vulnerable to the tide of God's will. We devise elaborate schemes to beat the odds, the aging process. We construct medical plans to defeat disease and build structures to hold back life's disappointments. When will we realize that God wants us to build castles, but castles of stone and not of sand, our lives on Stone not sand.

As a child I learned the children's chorus based on Jesus' parable: "A foolish man built his house upon the sand . . . a wise man built his house upon a rock . . . So build your life upon the Lord Jesus Christ and the blessings will come down!" Until you recognize that it is only when you build a life on Christ will you be fully secure from the tide of time.

71.

BEAUTIFUL BREEZES

A sea breeze contains a tang like no other breeze. An ocean breeze is salty and savory and stirs the natural senses like no other wind. The wind off a water invigorates and refreshes the entire being of man. Over the years I have been rejuvenated by these beautiful breezes "from sea to shining sea" and from shore to shore around the world.

These beautiful breezes will blow your hair around, rustle the trees along the shoreline, and gracefully tickle the grass. The lapping of the tides, the sonnets of the surf, and the singing of the shore birds are all caught by the breeze and blended together into a symphony that not only tantalizes the ear and brightens the eye, but brushes the face with its gentle touch. A beach breeze not only has wings, it also has a touch and a taste. Who of us hasn't felt the cooling, soothing touch of the breeze blowing in from the sea? Who of us hasn't felt the therapeutic, tingling touch of a wind off the ocean? Breezes touch your arm, the back of your leg, and the middle of your back with a calming massage that relaxes and restores your entire body. Sea air will brighten your cheek, calm your muscles, and soften your skin. What a sensation there is when the beautiful breeze from the beach engulfs you with its exhilaration energy.

Created far off shore, these beautiful breezes also have a marvellous taste. Spawned over salty water there is not only a freshness involved, but a cleanliness in these breezes. This salty air surrounds us as we walk the strand of sand we call home. For me home is in the state of Maine, but for others, those I have had the privilege to visit, like in India, the bit of beach is found along Kerala's western shoreline. Sea breezes off the Arabian Sea are warm compared to the cool breezes off the Gulf of Maine. Wonderfully wholesome is a fitting description of these Kerala breezes. I have had the wonderful honor of inhaling on that seashore three times now, one of my favorite destinations in all of India. The feeling of that pure (no pollution there) breeze entering my lungs is a wonderful high. The high levels of oxygen formed over the sea provide an extraordinary amount of breathable air that rushes its life-giving oxygen into the blood stream. It courses through the circulatory system recharging and refreshing like no other place. Your energy level spikes and you feel young again! I tell people that when I am in India I feel like a kid, a boy of my youth. I think part of the reason is the beautiful breezes I get to breathe.

To stand on a sea shore and breathe deeply a sea breeze is one of those alive moments. Invisible for sure, but the impact those beautiful breezes have on your entire being is almost divine. Remember it was a breath that gave life to mankind (Genesis 2:7). And every breath of air is controlled by the Almighty. Remember the day Jesus and His disciples were in a storm on the Sea of Galilee? It simply says: "Then He arose, and rebuked the winds and the sea; and there was a great calm. But the men marveled saying, what manner of man is this, that even the winds [breezes] and sea obey Him!" (Matthew 8:26-27) These breezes might be inexhaustible, invisible, and immense, but they are controlled despite their enormous impact. Their exposure to us can be frightening, but they can also be refreshing. We can stand in reverence to its power, but we can also be rejuvenated by the properties it carries that help us. These breezes will run their fingers through my hair, kiss my cheeks, and touch my face with a tenderness of a loving mother. As we walk along the source of those breezes, we are made alive, we are energized, we are restored to the way we were in our younger days. I have come to believe these beautiful breezes are the breath of God on all of us.

72.

PEACEFUL PLACES

Some of the most peaceful places I have ever experienced were by a sea of water. If you have found such a bit of beach by the ocean's edge, you know what I am writing about. A strip of shoreline that runs along a ribbon of rugged coastline that contains a sandy, rocky strand of sand overlooked by a beautiful bluff contains a small piece of precious peace, a tranquil tranquility that sooths the soul and satisfies the spirit.

I have found my peaceful places in Maine, California, New Jersey, Alaska, Australia, Israel, and numerous other places. Beaches contain shining sand and rugged rocks on which rests the quiet repose of peace, the gentle contentment of quietness, the atmosphere of serenity, and the interlude of concord. It is the same peace I have always found along the gentle brooks of my youth or the streams of my boyhood. Any place that contains water, big waters like an ocean or small waters like a lake, have brought great tranquility to me. Many places of peace are located near busy places, people places, the clamor of civilization, but because of the water these places stand apart as places of peace. My brother's Jersey shore house is one such place. Packed in like sardines, the houses on Long Beach Island are mere feet apart, but once you're on the other side of the sand dunes, peace. The high ramparts of the Jersey shore dunes stand as a guard against the fast-paced metropolis just on the other side of the sand. Traffic sounds, siren sounds, people sounds, auto sounds, and bustling business sounds disappear on the other side, muffled by the crashing of surf and the bellowing of the breeze. Caught up in the sights and the site, all is lost against the overwhelming feeling of tranquility.

The event that brought me to this repose in my life was the death of my son. Death loves to defeat peace. Dying more often than not comes with disturbing images and heart-felt sorrow, both not conducive to harmony of soul and mind. But enfolded in the endless sea and the eternal breeze, the heart begins to calm and the mind begins to quiet. The wind action and the wave action begin to allow concord between the loss and the joy that came when Scott was no longer suffering. The beach breezes breathe a renewed serenity and a needful strength back into your life. Slowly but surely peace begins to return and this peaceful place, this secluded and private place, begins the process of getting you back to a new normal that life will go on, must go on, and peace can be found again. The peace of a sea edge walk will allow you to become lost in your thoughts, but in those thoughts you will find the words of God that were put there years ago coming back to your heart and with them ". . . the peace that passes all understanding . . ." (Philippians 4:7) It was then I remembered a proverb of the wise man Solomon, and for the first time in my life I understood its meaning: "Yea, thou shalt be as he that lieth down in the midst of the sea, or as he that lieth upon the top of a mast." (Proverbs 23:34)

Was that not what Jesus did one day as He and His disciples crossed the Sea of Galilee? "And when He was entered into the ship, His disciples followed Him. And, behold, there arose a great tempest in the sea, insomuch that the ship was covered with the waves: but he was asleep." (Matthew 8:23-24) Only an amazing internal peace would allow such a nap in the midst of a sea. My family and I were in the midst of a cancer storm, a storm that claimed my son and was drowning my wife, our daughter, and me. Yet like Jesus I can honestly say that along the white beaches of Long Beach Island I found a peace of mind, a tranquility of heart, and repose in a sacred communion with my Creator. I found a peaceful place, and I am persuaded it is open to all who will visit.

73.

TRANQUIL TIDES

One doesn't have to be a monk in a monastery, a saint in a sanctuary, a recluse sitting by a river, or a mystic on a mountain to enjoy the amazing world the good Lord has given us. There is nothing sinful or evil about being drawn into God's environment, and there is nothing wrong if a certain section of Creation casts a spell on your heart. The wrong comes when we see the creation over the Creator, and we worship the creation above the Creator (Romans 1:20-23). Whether you are a barelegged tourist on the beaches of Florida or an old gentleman strolling the soft sand of Kerala at sunset, the contentment found at such times isn't wrong. It is a marvelous gift of God just like the tranquility of the tides.

I only lived five years with the tides. Oh, I still live on the coast of Maine, but the tides that roll in and out of the Union River don't affect my life like they use to when I was surrounded by the Gulf of Maine in Passamaquoddy Bay. It was my tour of duty on Moose Island that taught me about the tranquil tides, often a word not used to describe the gravity-affected water of the ocean. I only lived five years with the Passamaquoddy tides, but I can say after 66 years living somewhere Moose Island had a greater tranquility than any other place I have lived including my beloved homestead in northern Maine or my "church of a lifetime" in Ellsworth, Maine. The tranquility of Eastport settled in your soul just like a seagull settles on an old pier post sticking out of Eastport harbor. The beauty of this tranquility is found in the gentle (sometimes not so gentle) rocking of the water back and forth, daily, monthly, yearly in a rhythm that God created and put within the structure of His marvellous masterpiece we call creation. Once man discovered the secret of the tides, once he could chart the ins and outs and the ups and downs, he was able to fish and live and be in harmony with the sea.

The warm air above it, or sometimes the Arctic air over it, or the soft breezes in from it, or sometimes the gales that invade it, or the drift of sea fog that often enfolds it, or the rain clouds that sometimes engulf it, the tide is never affected by anything and with that unchanging nature comes a sweet quietude. I sat for hours on Greenlaw Beach during my half decade of service to the Washington Street Baptist Church and just watched the advancing tide or the retreating tide. Granted, it is like watching the sun in its course in the sky changing so slowly you might get bored, but with the tide there is the scenic seascape, the animal life in the bay, the busy boats as they come and go, Campobello Island in the distance, and countless other sights and sites to see. It is not just the tide that brings a tranquility of heart and mind, but I found on Moose Island the most laid back human beings on this planet. The only other people that even come close to the inhabitants of Eastport are the people of Edayappara, my home town in Kerala, India. The hours I spent watching and witnessing the change of the tide was such a healing for me, both physically and spiritual. I came to Moose Island physically tired and spiritual drained, but I left there with the means to take on a 26-year pastorate in Ellsworth.

The only spiritual illustration I can think off are the meals the angel prepared for the discouraged Elijah, meals that allowed him to travel forty days and forty nights to the Mount of God (I Kings 19:5-8). I also found this phrase in the Book of Daniel: ". . . if it may be a lengthening of thy tranquility." (Daniel 4:27) The tranquility of the tides is a placid virtue that only God can give (John 14:27); a peace that will last for eternity, a serenity as timeless as the tides, as predictable as the seas, and as calming as the hand of God.

74.

BEACH BOY

I have just returned from my fifth trip to California in the last two years. The reason for those trips has been a blue-eyed, dark-headed, brown-skinned (his father is Mexican) lad named Judah Alan. My wife and I arrived in 2015 just as he was being born and have returned in August ever since to celebrate his birth, with a couple of trips in between. This trip was to celebrate Judah's second birthday and to spend some time with the apple of our eye, my daughter Marnie, who is expecting her second child early next year. Our two weeks together were filled with parties and plenty of play. Needless to say, Judah's play patterns have changed dramatically from the year before. I learned very early in our stay just how difficult it was for a 66-year old to keep up with a two-year old!

During our stay Marnie, Judah, and I took a day to go to Fort Ord Beach while GiGi (Judah's name for his grandmother) took a day to rest. Coleen also discovered just how tiring a two year old could be at sixty-five! Located on Monterey Bay this beach is on the western side of a massive, former Army training base. Stretching into the inner harbor of Monterey, the beach runs for miles up the Pacific Coast of California. Our destination for this beach adventure was a small section of beach lined to the east by huge Cypress trees and connected to a large boardwalk on its southern end. We parked the car on a busy Monterey street by a small park used mostly for sunning and walking your dog. There were plenty of flowering bushes and one big concrete blue whale ("And God created great whales . . ." Genesis

1:21) rising up through a sand pit with a massive starfish next door. This play structure was the first stop on our morning at the sea shore.

As we walked toward the play area, I spotted Canadian geese (a favorite) feeding on the green lawn leading to the beach. Judah stopped for a few minutes reintroducing himself to a favorite play place, according to his mother, but his interest and mine soon drew us to the beach. I had been on bigger beaches, deeper beaches, and busier beaches, but that morning I was just thankful to add another amazing beach to the list of beaches I have had the privilege of visiting. There was a dense fog just off shore so you couldn't see far into the Pacific, but far enough to see plenty of seabirds, a few sailing ships bobbling in the light surf, and the rippling waves. The breeze was warm and the beach was nearly deserted. Marnie said it was because school was back in session.

Our walk down Fort Ord Beach to the boardwalk was a meandering affair as Judah switched from throwing rocks into the surf to digging holes in the sand. I was looking for shells but found none, but what I found on Fort Ord Beach were soft stones in which small sea snails had made holes. It was unique for me having never seen it before, but what I had seen and was always excited to find was sea glass. We picked about two dozen pieces, mostly green and white in color. Eventually we made it to the boardwalk and started our trip to the end. Along the way I stopped to visit with an elderly fisherman who was looking to catch anything, and we watched some younger fishermen chase a small school of mackerel from one end of the pier to the other. We did see one man hook one, but lost it as he tried to pull it up from ocean to railing (about a thirty foot pull). Our short time on Fort Ord Beach ended back at the whale where Judah lingered, crawling through the gap made by the massive tail and the main body emerging from the sand. Judah also enjoyed jumping from the starfish into the sand. It was then I realized that like his grandfather, Judah was going to be a beach boy.

75.

SEA SOUNDS

After visiting for the first time Fort Ord Beach in Monterey, California, I was struck with the truth of why God created the sea creatures and the air creatures on the same day: "And God blessed them, saying, be fruitful and multiply, and fill the waters in the seas, and let the fowl multiply in the earth. And the evening and the morning were the fifth day." (Genesis 1:22-23) Granted, there are plenty of birds that never see the ocean, but how many are there that do?

One of the things I love best about the sea shore is its sounds. When I speak of quietness, it isn't that I want silence. Even when I sleep I like a sound. What I love best are the natural sounds God created, not the artificial sounds of man. To listen to the voices of the beach, especially the whispers, is a joy beyond compare. As Judah, Marnie, and I strolled onto Fort Ord Beach the sounds of the city behind faded; that is what the sea can do, mute and muffle the sound of people, traffic, and civilization. As we worked our way down the Pacific Highway toward Monterey, I watched the huge breakers crash into the California coast, but by the time we got down to Fort Ord Beach the surf was light because of the shelter and refuge created by Monterey Bay. So as we walked the edge of the sea looking for sea glass and seashells, the waves were barely able to climb the slight rise of the sand. I learned long ago that the seashore can make many sounds. The accents and the notes played by sea on sand and wind over waves along a strip of shore are like a musical instrument except God is the musician, and He plays some of the most amazing music ever composed in the universe.

The sounds of the sea, the murmuring of the tide, the notes of the birds, the thundering of the waves, the softness of the sea creatures, the lapping of the surf, and the movement of liquid over land all contribute to the symphony of the sea. The day we climbed the dunes and hiked the beach off Monterey Bay, the sounds were blending into a wonderful cantata. I don't know what Marnie was hearing or Judah was picking up, but for me it was a marvellous concert of sounds. Running water and bird sounds have for my entire life been a calming time for me. This past spring I purchased my very first water feature for our porch. The two-tub item is simply water dropping twice before being recycled, but those two drops of water into water is heavenly to me. I have spent more time on our porch this summer than any other, and I believe it is simply because of the sound of falling water. Whether falling or washing up on a sandy beach, add to that the sound of birds, land birds or sea birds, makes no difference. I believe on the fifth day of creation God was doing more than designing fish and birds. He was also creating a sort of solace and solitude for the man He would create the next day. He knew that man would instinctively be drawn to the sea when he heard the voices of His fifth day creation and would be inspired, as I have been through this series of sermonettes.

Once again the walk with my grandson along Fort Ord Beach refreshed me, and it was part of the rejuvenation I got in California. The loveliness of the sea sounds I heard was not diminished by the gray skies that hung over the scene. If anything, the low hanging clouds and the sea fog off shore only amplified the still small sounds that morning. The echo of the sea birds flying low over the water's edge was clearer to me. The soft surf was more intense, like when the conductor softens the brass section and tunes up the stringed section. There was no clash of cymbals that day at Fort Ord Beach, just a series of sea sounds that were an enormous stimulus and a splendid memory to me.

76.

WAVE WRECKAGE

One of the things that fascinate me most about my walks along a beach is the wave wreckage that washes up on the sand. Over my years of walking the sandy stretches of sea shore I have had the privilege of visiting the leftovers from something wrecked at sea. It might be as simple as a small piece of glass broken from a bottle cast into the sea a few months before, or it might be as large as a piece of wood from a wreaked sailing ship of centuries ago. I wondered years ago the first time I read of Paul's ship wreck on the shores of Malta if any of his ship remains: "And falling into a place where two seas met, they ran the ship aground; and the forepart stuck fast, and remained unmoveable, but the hinder part was broken with the violence of the waves." (Acts 27:41)

I have long been amazed with the leftovers of a storm. A bit of timber, where did it come from? Was it a piece from an old sailing ship that broke up in the sea off the coast of Maine because of a "nor'easter" like with Paul (Acts 27:14) a hundred years ago? Or a length of rope, where did it come from? Was it an anchor rope, a sail rope, or a rope off a lobster trap? Or a broken bottle, who had cast it into the sea? Had it come from a far off land or from a ship, or maybe at one time it contained a message and the paper had been lost? Most shorelines I have explored contain its share of wave wreckage. Each piece has its own story, but very few stories are ever told by the silent piece of wreckage because the sea, sand, time, and tides have destroyed any link to the source of the story. What I have learned on my seaside strolls and the wave wreckage is that there are many similarities along the shore of humanity and wrecked lives.

Having been in the people business of pastoring for 44 years now, I too have come across many broken fragments of humanity, people who tried to resist the divine will of God by building their strong ships and crafty crafts of self will. In their stubborn determination (check Acts 27:9-11) they have set sail on the sea of life only to be broken apart by the stress and strain of countless storms that have left them scattered on the beach of life. Think of what happened to Jonah when he tried to run from God (Jonah 1). When I have come across them, they are but pieces of hopeless life. They are only a shell of their former glory when they set sail with grand expectations and wonderful anticipation of what they would do. After the storm, there were only bits and pieces left of their hopes and dreams. Each thought their strong will was strong enough to take the pounding of an ocean of self ambition. They thought themselves secure behind their sea walls of stocks, bonds, and insurance they created to protect themselves. (I write this in the wake of Hurricane Harvey.) Each thought their ships were powerful enough and their walls big enough to restrain the waves of despair, disappointment, and distress. Granted, some took a lot of abuse before they sank, but like Paul's ship to Rome eventually the sea was too strong and the storm too long. Finally, caught in the cross fire of wave upon wave, bit by bit their lives were broken apart and left to drift to the nearest beach.

Yet it is there on that lonely strand of sand the Master Collector is walking daily. He is looking for wave wreckage. He is looking for wrecked lives. He is looking for brokenness and weariness. Unlike the pieces of wreckage I have found on the beaches of my life, God knows your story. He knows what you have been through, the journey you have been on. He knows like He knew with Zacchaeus (Luke 19:1-10) your name and your need. He has watched you fall apart and drift to His beach of grace. He has been waiting your arrival. Jesus is the answer to your wrecked life (Jonah 3:1).

77.

TIDE TREASURE

As I watched the beachcombers stroll and stoop their way across the strand of sand we were calling home for a few days, I asked my traveling companions the Clarks, "What are these beach walkers doing?" Danny and Lori replied, "They are looking for treasures between the tides!" Their response provoked this sermonette based on this phrase from Deuteronomy 33:19: ". . . and of the treasures hid in the sand."

"Treasures between the tides," I asked. "What kind of treasure?" The answer was clear enough, but the spiritual application goes a bit deeper. Shells and shark's teeth for selling were the quests of the Florida flocks I saw on Nokomis Beach and Casperson Beach along the Sunshine State's seashore. It was my first time to Florida, and it was my first experience with beachcombers with a purpose. As I walked through the gathering tide, I observed them raking and pawing the sand for small treasures deposited by the last high tide, the last surge of the sea. I witnessed an elderly lady pick up a bright, odd-shaped shell. She washed the clinging sand off in the salty water and felt its strange form between her fingers. You could tell from the expression on her face that she admired the object that she had found. It was placed softly and gently into a bag she was carrying at her waist. She then moved on still searching for another treasure, or she hadn't found what she was looking for. I watched another shell hunter as he discovered a delicate shell that had somehow survived the pounding surf. Its special shape hadn't been damaged, and the hues of its colors were lovely in the reflective sunlight now shining brightly on the beach. I could see in his eyes why he had been drawn to this treasure from between the tides.

As I took my walk down the beach, I pondered on the concept being played out before my eyes as the beachcombers pressed on in their searching. A number of spiritual principles clearly came to mind. First, the treasure hunter had to pay close attention or he or she would miss the treasure. Often half buried in the sand, the shell or shark's tooth was not always clearly visible, and so it is with God's Word and will. You must always keep a sharp spiritual eye. Second, it takes time and patience to cover the amount of beach necessary to find one treasure. I thought of the parables of the treasure in the field (Matthew 13:44) and the Pearl of Great Price (Matthew 13:45-46). Third, it takes some thought and forethought of just what you are looking for. My wife and I tried to find both shells and shark's teeth which we did, but none worth much other than a keepsake from our time on the beaches of Florida. You could tell the true hunters knew what they were looking for, and they knew when to search between the surf. What are you looking for?

Like the shells and shark's teeth on Nokomis and Casperson Beaches, the treasures of God's Word and will aren't always obvious, yet they are there. They can be found if you know what you are looking for and are patience, persevering, paying attention, and staying alert. Like the treasures between the tides, there are treasures between the pages of God's Word. Scriptural treasures are, however, only found when the reader (Revelation 1:3 and I Timothy 4:13) pays attention (no daydreaming or you will miss the blessing), practice patience in reading (it might be your fifth time through before you see it), and know what you are looking for. Like the seekers on the sand, you must not race over the pages of Holy Writ. You must plod and probe every word, sentence, verse, and chapter. Just like the beachcombers, you must be a Biblecomber. Ours must be a deliberate search, and, if we are willing to take the time and apply what we already know, we too will return from our hunt with an eternal treasure that was placed in the tide of time just for us. It is there!

78.

SMOOTH SAND

I know nothing of the makeup of sand, but this I know: it is smooth once the tide rolls over it. Its shape might be altered by building sand castles with it or sea walls called dunes and silly shapes on its surface, but the minute the waves return and the sea surge surges over it for just a few times, it will return to its former smooth self. I might even mark it with my footprints and leave the imprint of my shoes across its face, but once the ocean reclaims its high water mark, any evidence that I walked across it will be wiped clean and a fresh canvas of smooth sand will be laid by the turning of the tide. Job would say in his classic defense against the false accusations of his friends, "For now it would be heavier than the sand of the sea: therefore my words are swallowed up." (Job 6:3)

Such is the reality of a new day in anybody's life. Each one is as fresh and clean as the newly formed beach of pure sand on any shoreline in the world. Time like the tide can give us a new start or a second chance, if we allow it. Why did Jesus tell us not to borrow from tomorrow (Matthew 6:34) or fret about yesterday? He proclaimed the truth of smooth sand when He spoke of each day being enough to handle and to take care of. By the washing of His grace He too can smooth over those bad marks that leave a scar on your yesterday. Sometimes when you see a stretch of sand walked over by hundreds, dug up by the wheels of jeeps, and littered by the ocean, you wonder if anything can clean up the mess. But overnight with the turn of the tide, by the next morning that same stretch of beach is just smooth sand. Jesus can forgive the marring of sin and He can wash away iniquity making you whiter than snow (Isaiah 1:18). Jesus can also smooth the surface of our lives, and it will appear as if sin hasn't walked all over us because He forgives and forgets. How most of us still need to learn the lesson of smooth sand. How we need to see each day as a clean canvas, ready to be used for God's glory and our good. This too shall pass away, but only if we allow the tide of God's mercy to roll over our sand castles of self will and sea walls of self gratification. Let His marvelous smoothing waves of love transform our marked and marred spirit into a smoother life.

Like with life, the seashore never remains the same. As I return time after time to my favorite beaches, I notice the change in the patterns of the sands. There have been storms since my last visit that affect the sand. In some places the depth of the sand has changed, the width of the beach has changed, or the contour of the seashore has changed. Then there are the sea birds walking here and there that leave their marks. The wind plays its part as does the water from the sea. Yet each works in harmony and unity to design the smooth strand of sand into its own unique form. Surely you have never seen two beaches the same. So does the Master Conductor of our lives. God has never promised that our lives won't be touched by storm (John 16:33). He has never promised that Satan will not leave his mark on our lives (I Peter 5:8). The good Lord has never promised that the wind of adversity will not blow over our beach (Acts 14:22), but He has promised that in time He will smooth it all out for our good (Romans 8:28). All things will be smooth for them that love God and are called according to His purpose. Today you might be walking in rough sand, stony sand, or shell-infested sand. The walking is difficult and the trip between the tides is nearly impossible. Be patient. The tide of God's love and grace is in the bay ready to sweep your strand of sand clean and smooth. On the average beach this is done by the ocean, but for us it is the overflowing blood of Christ (I John 1:7). Before you know it, two sets of footprints will be seen walking side by side over the smooth sand.

79.

TITANIC TRANSACTION

Until I moved to Moose Island off the downeast seacoast of Maine, I knew nothing of the titanic transaction that took place between the ocean and the seashore every day, a mighty interchange that goes on without fanfare, fuss, or flair. I believe the Psalmist defined this transaction best when he wrote, "Thy way is in the sea, and Thy path in the great waters, and Thy footsteps are not seen." (Psalm 77:19)

Every day the sea washes over the dirty beach of the seashore and picks up that which stains the sand. In place of polluted soil it leaves behind a polished place. It is the breakers of the tide that clean the beach. It is the waves of the sea that washes clean the shore. When the tide retreats to its resting place, it leaves a restored land. I use to watch this transaction on my lunch hour when I would drive to Greenlaw Beach for munching and meditation. It was there I pondered the great parallels between the sea and the soul, between the land and the Lord, and between the beach and the body.

Like the land along Greenlaw Beach, my life needs continual and constant cleaning. I need to be washed in the daily forgiveness of Christ. (Ephesians 1:7) Sins collect in my life on a daily bases, and if it were not for the cleansing flow of Christ's blood (I John 1:7) through my life, I would be polluted beyond measure or imagination. Like the beach with the daily rising tide, I need not resist the overflowing grace of God upon my life. Greenlaw Beach knows it is for its benefit that the waters of Passamaquoddy Bay return twice a day. I too know it is good for me that God's grace returns, surges through me on a regular basis, and that His love is still being applied. There is a peace on Greenlaw Beach that knows no matter the strength of the tide, the tide will clean and purify. There is a peace that comes to the believer when he or she realizes that there is a forgiving force more powerful than any debris of sin, stronger than any dirty iniquity, and mightier than any demon the devil can attack us with. When I was a kid, I had the privilege of learning numerous choruses that have stayed with me into my sixties, and the theology of these choruses have also been a great source of help to me. One such chorus was written by Helen Gripps and goes like this: "Gone, gone, gone, gone! Yes, my sins are gone! Now my soul is free and in my heart's a song! Buried in the deepest sea! Yes, that's good enough for me! I shall live eternally! Praise God my sins are gone, gone, gone, gone!"

Where did those things from Greenlaw Beach go? Where do my sins go? The Hebrew prophet Micah tells us, "He will turn again, He will have compassion upon us; He will subdue our iniquities; and thou wilt cast all our sins into the depths of the sea." (Micah 7:19) The sea is a depository for a lot of things, and even in the spiritual realm there is a place. The verse from the Psalms that inspired this sermonette from the seashore tells us that God has a way in the sea, a path in the ocean, yet His footsteps are not seen. Why? Because nobody can follow Him to the place He has buried our sins. The reason they are unknown is because they go to the resting place of our sins, forgiven, forgotten, forever. All our sins and all our mistakes are taken far away (Psalm 103:12) into the depth of the sea. As the tide takes the grime and garbage and transports it away into the fathomless deep of the ocean, I believe the good Lord also taken our sins and stains and carries them to a place that only He knows about and soon forgets about. I believe Philip Doddridge put this theology into verse many years ago when he wrote: "Tis done: the great transaction's done, I am the Lord's and He is mine; He drew me and I followed on, charmed to confess the voice divine. Happy day, happy day, when Jesus washed my sins away!"

80.

FOOTSTEP FOOTPRINT

Over the years I have planted my footsteps on many beaches. My last was just a week ago when I made footprints on Fort Ord Beach on the coast of Monterey, California, with my grandson Judah and his mother Marnie. Often as I walk along some sandy shore I look back on the tracks I have made, and without a doubt I remember a favorite and now famous writing of many years ago. I have never found out who the author is, but the story told has touched my heart in so many ways and every so often in my life. Do you recall?

> "One night a man had a dream. He dreamed he was walking along a beach with the Lord. Across the sky flashed scenes from his life. For each scene, he noticed two sets of footprints in the sand; one belonging to him, and the other to the Lord. When the last scene of his life flashed before him, he looked back at the footprints in the sand. He noticed that many times along the path of his life there was only one set of footprints. He also noticed that it happened at the very lowest and saddest times in his life. This really bothered him and he questioned the Lord about it. 'Lord, you said that once I decided to follow you, you'd walk with me all the way. But I have noticed that during the most troublesome times of my life, there is only one set of footprints. I don't understand why when I needed you most you would leave me?' The Lord replied, 'My precious, precious child, I love you and I would never leave

you. During your times of trial and suffering, when you see only one set of footprints, it was then that I carried you!'"

What a profound Biblical truth is found in this sermonette from a sea shore. Amen!

Only a beach walker can fully understand the implications of this simple tale, but only a Bible reader can fully comprehend the Scripture truth contained in the prose. The first truth that is revealed is the great promise of Hebrews 13:5-6: ". . . for He hath said, I will never leave thee not forsake thee. So that we may boldly say, The Lord is my helper, and I will not fear what man shall do unto me." Often when I stroll along some stretch of sand like I did on Long Beach Island in New Jersey after my son's passing, I often look to my right or left and think I see another set of footprints. I never felt Him nearer than in those *lowest and saddest* days, and I know that I would have never made it through that cancer walk with Scott without "Him carrying me."

But the Biblical appeal that best describes the lines quoted above is this thought from the pen of "the sweet psalmist of Israel," (II Samuel 23:1) David: "Hold up my goings in Thy paths, that my footsteps slip not." (Psalm 17:5) It is a sad state of affairs today when most choose to walk life's beaches on their own, even many Christians. Why? Why would you walk alone when Jesus will walk with you and carry you when needed?

81.

CALIFORNIA COAST

"*. . . and from the sea coast of . . .*" (Luke 6:17) This phrase comes from the travel log of Jesus recorded by Luke, but I too have such a phrase to highlight.

On the coast of central California where my daughter and family live pleasant weather prevails the year around, or so says my son-in-law, Josue Legaspi. Josue believes he lives in the best place in the world where the weather never gets too cold or too hot and where the climate is predictable throughout the year. Where most have four seasons, the Salinas Valley only seems to have one. Twenty miles from Monterey Bay, the town of Salinas has for most of the year a truly Mediterranean climate. I have been there five times now, and I will have to admit no matter the month the weather is the same. Granted, it might be foggy in the morning, but rare has been the day that Mr. Sun (after a song my grandson likes: "Oh, Mr. Sun, Sun, Mr. Golden Sun . . .") hasn't made an appearance, and rarely is the region wrapped in rain and dampness. What makes this possible is the California coastline to the west of town. As the Atlantic coast affects our weather in Ellsworth (also just twenty miles from the ocean) so the Pacific coast affects their weather. For us the nearness of the sea makes us cooler in the summer and warmer in the winter. The vastness and size of the Pacific keeps that particular section of California moderate all year around.

Occasionally, storms will surge out of the Pacific laden with subtropical moisture, and when these rains come (like they did early in the year of

2017), heavy deluges cover the valley. Very quickly the excess waters gather in every stream, many of them just sundrenched creeks for most of the year. But on those rare events, these trenches suddenly fill with cascading flood waters and fill the slow lying areas. Because Salinas is surrounded by field after field covered in lettuce and strawberries in season, the water slowly sinks into the land and collects in the massive aquifer under the valley. Our trip there in April revealed an Eden with everything green, but by the time we got there in August for Judah's second birthday it was brown again like it is most of the time, or at least the times we have been there. Oh, the irrigated fields are green, green because of the life-giving rains that came months before, and all this is because of the California coast.

As I thought of the contrast on the coast of California, I thought of my own contrast in my two visits in 2017. In August the landscape and seascape reflected and matched my melancholy mood of my inner spirit in April following the death of my father and my 39-year old son. I was grieved and torn, troubled and broken. We had gone to the New Jersey shore first for a week and then off to California for a week to recover from the shock and be reassured that our Father knows best. And then by August, our spirit was more like the green and spring of the California coast. The air was refreshing, and the climate was like my new mood. I had come to grips with my son's departure and my father's death. I knew that God was still on the throne, and He was working all things to His glory and my good (Romans 8:28). The sun was out again, the crops were growing in the fields again, the rains had passed, and the rainbow had reappeared—an eternal promise that the storm had passed (Genesis 9:12-16). As I concluded my second trip to the California coast in just five months, I heard again the still small voice of God speak clearly to my heart, "I AM still with you. I will see you and yours through the rest of this trauma."

For every stormy and wintry Maine coast in our lives, the Almighty provided for us a sunny and seasonable California coast to rest, be restored, and feel renewed.

82.

SEA SONGS

I would be the first to tell you that I am no expert on the sea or anything dealing with the ocean, but this I do know from my many trips to the sea shore is that the sea sings a variety of songs.

The voice of the sea is much different than the voice of the forest. They sing different songs. The songs of the sea also vary depending on the mood of the water and the accent of the wind. Depending on where you stand to listen, you might get a different melody each time you go to your special piece of shoreline. If you go to the seaside on the coast of Maine, the granite cliffs and bluffs will affect the aria. If it is the season of shore birds, the harmony will also be much different between the varieties of elements on the seashore. For some they only hear the noise, but for those of us who have learned to listen, there is a sweet blending of tones between the wind and the waves, the birds and the bluffs, the granite and the ground, the sea and the shore. We often forget that Moses, the great deliverer of Israel, sang his first song about the sea: "Then sang Moses and the children of Israel this song unto the Lord, and spake, saying, I will sing unto the Lord, for he hath triumphed gloriously: the horse and his rider hath he thrown into the sea." (Exodus 15:1)

The sounds of the sea will also affect its songs depending on what shore you are standing on. I remember clearly a different song in Florida than I heard in Australia, California, or Israel. Even in my home state of Maine, the songs are different in Eastport versus Ellsworth, but one ingredient seems to be the same, whether local or foreign, sea songs sing sea sermons to my soul. There is a balm that comes from the beach song. There is a therapy that comes from the tide song. There is a restfulness that comes from a rising sea song. There is a peace that comes from a polyphony of sea songs. I know not what God calls them, but I know the good Lord is the composer of them. The song writer of all sea songs is the Creator Himself, and it is for us that He has designed and programmed the sea to sing. Could I share with you some of my favorites, my top twelve if you will? Let me count them down for you:

12. A rippling concert of waves crashing on Fort Ord Beach off Monterey Bay.
11. A soft song of peaceful interlude on Long Beach Island Beach in New Jersey.
10. A seaside serenade of seagulls and spruce trees off Shacksford Head in Eastport.
9. A potpourri of winds and waves off Sail Rock near Campobello Island.
8. A musical melody of rocks and rough seas at Thunder Hole in Acadia National Park.
7. A tune of terns and sand pipers on Casperson Beach in Florida.
6. A composition of blustery breezes and birch covered bluffs on Greenlaw Beach.
5. A harmony of breakwater and boats in Eastport Harbor.
4. A strain of sea and sand blending together on Nokomis Beach on the Gulf Coast.
3. A symphony of children's voices and a gathering storm off Herring Cove.
2. A sonata of surf and turf on Old Orchard Beach in Maine.
1. A simple measure of one wave lapping on shore off Melbourne Beach in Australia.

I would challenge you the next time you head for the shore and find yourself confronted by God's sea songs that you stand for a moment and open your ear to the music God has imbedded in the sea. You might just find a song worth hearing, a sermon worth remembering, and a sermonette worth writing about.

83.

WAVE WORK

I am a wave watcher, and have been ever since the good Lord redirected my life from the hills and hollows of Aroostook County to the coast of Maine. In my 66 years, I have lived 31 years on the shoreline of Downeast Maine (I only lived 30 years in the county of my birth; the other five years I lived in New Hampshire). It was there I learned to watch the tides of Passamaquoddy Bay. I love nothing better now than to find some peaceful place along the sea side and just watch the waves roll on shore. Only watching a campfire gives me more solace. There is something therapeutic about waves, whether seeing them or hearing them. The Hebrew Psalmist said it better when he wrote, "For He commandeth, and raiseth the stormy wind, which lifteth up the waves thereof." (Psalm 107:25)

It wasn't until I moved to an island off the downeast coast of Maine in the village of Eastport that I was able to enjoy this pleasure daily. There was a narrow country lane below the parsonage of the Washington Street Baptist Church that snaked its way around the inland side of Moose Island. They had closed the road off while expanding the Eastport airport during my five year stay on the island. I never kept track of how often I walked that road to enjoy the waves at work, but those strolls along that shoreline were memorable as you will see. I would periodically stop along my walk just to watch the sea break on shore or simply watch the rising of the tide whether carrying large wave or wavelets. The sound of those waves crashing against the granite-lined shore still echoes in my ear as I write this sermonette. The rolling, rhythmic rise of the sea currents can almost hypnotize you. One only has to put up with the smell in the summertime of the empty mudflats before the waves work their magic and all disappears under a flood of ocean water. What a privilege to watch the waves work themselves towards you.

    I especially enjoyed sitting on the gigantic granite stones at the breakwater in Eastport Harbor as the waves would roll in at high tide. Being on the sea side of the island, the waves were usually larger than the ones in the bay near the parsonage. These harbor waves would hit the shore with more force and even harder when there was a gale up. The oscillating movement of the waves creates a calming atmosphere even in the midst of a storm. Like the campfire I wrote of above, the sound of the waves works its way into your soul like the flames of a campfire. I have sat at times contemplating the force of the waves in awe of the might of the water and the rare strength of H_2O with a wind behind it. As the water rises higher and higher against the manmade breakwater, one wonders when it will stop or if it will stop. It is particularly impressive at high tide or an astronomic high tide. I have witnessed on the greater storms the waves in the sea beyond the pier were as high as me, and, when you consider the open ocean was beyond Campobello Island, this was amazing. The waves would throw water onto the huge dock and often into the boats tied to its many piers. The ocean seemed everywhere ready to engulf the sleepy coastal city. It would flow with rough swells over the rocks attempting to reach my observation stone. The waves would deposit debris of every sort among the cracks and crevices of the sea wall. Everything on the surface of the waves was flung against that breakwater, but I often ignored the junk as I focused on the pulse of the waves, back and forth, the swirling, surging greenish/blue water pounding the shore.

    It was during those days of watching the waves at work that I came to a closer relationship with the One that sets the waves in motion. Whether a powerful wave or a gentle wavelet, I heard God say, "This wave is for you to quiet your spirit and calm your soul..."

84.

BEACH BREAKERS

One of the reasons I love to walk the seashore is to reap the calming effect of the beach breakers. Most don't see the medicine found in the waves lapping on shore, but I do, and the Hebrew Psalmist who wrote these lines must have as well: "He maketh the storm a calm, so that the waves thereof are still." (Psalm 107:29)

The repeated roll of the sea over a strand of sand is calming to a troubled life, a stressful soul, or a distressed spirit. Its ability to block out other sounds and sights is amazing, transfixing! Once you fix your ear and eye on the incoming waves all else seems to fade away, disappear in the rhythm of the sea. Over and over and over again this simple message from the Bible comes into your mind and down into your heart. God has calmed the storm so that you can enjoy His stillness (Psalm 46:10). It is as if the waves are repeating this again and again, "I Love You. I Love You. I Love You. I Am Here For You. Let Me Calm Your Troubled Mind, And Let Me Calm Your Troubled Soul!"

Life and living in this present world (Titus 2:12) is sometimes like an ocean storm to the believer. There are those that believe that if we belong to God, there will be no storms, no troubled seas. Some think that we will be exempt from rough waves if we are in the Spirit, travelling with Jesus. Not so. (Don't forget the upright and righteous man Job.) Remember the times that Jesus and His disciples went to sea and the troubled waves and boisterous winds they encountered? The disciples even feared for their lives just like Job. Yes, we can be certain that on our journey through this storm-tossed life we will experience the winds of adversity and the gales of trouble. Sadness, sorrow, sickness, and separation (all experienced last year by my family and I with the cancer and ultimate death of our son Scott) will blow across our course, and we will hear the howling winds and feel the rocking waves of difficulty. They will roll over us trying to swamp or engulf our bark. Yet in the midst of every storm, as with the disciples, Jesus will be in our midst. His voice will call the wind to cease, and His presence will calm the waves. Then in a wonderful grace He will lead us to the sea shore, and we will bask in the calming breakers on the beach, just like my family and I did on Long Beach Island last spring.

Let us never forget that our constant and continual travelling companion is always involved in the storms of our life. A simple reading of Job 1-2 will highlight and underline this truth that nothing happens in a believer's life without God first giving permission. The storm that killed Job's ten children was God-sanctioned. It is He that has arranged the situations and circumstances that result in a storm that is ultimately for our strengthening, not our destruction. He, as with the disciples on the Sea of Galilee, is behind the scenes to walk with us even when we think He is not near. At other times He might seem to be asleep in the storm, but He is not (Psalm 121:4). He walks through the storm to join us in our plight, and He awakes in the midst of the storm to calm our fears. In the darkest hour He walks on the sea to guide our boat to the breakers of peace on the distant shore, and, at the height of the raging sea, He speaks, the storm ceases, and we are on a calm shore again. It is on that safe shore we hear again the splendid sound of beach breakers at the sea edge, and its music and melody softens the strain and stress of the passing storm in our soul, the haunting horror in our heart, and the sorrowful silence in our spirit. The once surging sea is quiet, and the only sound it has left is a whimper or a whisper, a calming whisper that sounds like a lullaby. The same waves that would have destroyed me are the same waves that restored my sanity.

85.

STILLING STORMS

"*And when He was entered into a ship, His disciples followed Him.*" (Matthew 8:23) Be assured of this, if you follow Jesus you will be led into the fury of a storm or two before you finish your cruise through this storm-tossed life. God never promised and His Son never taught a storm-free passage to "the haven of rest." He has promised: "He will not suffer thy foot to be moved: He that keepeth thee will not slumber." (Psalm 12:3) Remember Paul during that tremendous typhoon (Acts 27) in the midst of the Mediterranean Sea, and not only was Paul preserved, but all with him.

"*And, behold, there arose a great tempest in the sea, insomuch that the ship was covered with waves; but he was asleep.*" (Matthew 8:24) Be assured of this, when the worst storm of your life hits it will seem that the Almighty God is asleep. God never promised us a wave-free voyage to the heavenly dock. He has promised: "Behold, He that keepeth Israel shall neither slumber nor sleep." (Psalm 121:4) So how do we explain Jesus sleeping? I see it this way. Jesus in His humanity had to sleep, but His Father wasn't asleep so the disciples were perfectly safe in a boat. As someone once said, "No boat can sink with the Son of Man in it even if it is 'covered with waves.'"

"*And His disciples came to Him, and awoke Him, saying, Lord, save us: we perish.*" (Matthew 8:25) Be assured of this, there will come a time in your life when your only hope will be to awaken the Lord through a petition. God has not promised us a fear-free trip to Glory's harbor. He has promised: "The Lord is thy keeper: the Lord is thy shade upon thy right hand."

(Psalm 121:5) No storm can stop a prayer, no gale can block a supplication, and no sea can impede an intercession. If you cry, He will hear, and when He hears, He will come to your side and calm your sea.

"*And He saith unto them, Why are ye fearful, oh ye of little faith?*" (Matthew 8:26) Be assured of this, a storm will come into your life that will test your faith in God and God alone. God has not promised us a trial-free journey to a safe anchorage. He has promised: "The sun shall not smite thee by day, nor the moon by night." (Psalm 121:6) Faith will be tested (I Peter 1:6) somehow and someday. Even the best of them had their faith tested in the fire of trial or in the case of the disciples the water of trial.

"*Then he arose, and rebuked the winds and the sea: and there was a great calm.*" (Matthew 8:26) Be assured of this, no matter how dangerous or difficult your storm, Jesus is ready, willing, and able to cast it aside and restore calmness to your sea. God has not promised us an agony-free jaunt to our eternal destination. He has promised: "The Lord shall preserve thee from all evil: He shall preserve thy soul." (Psalm 121:7) Note, "thy soul" not thy body as I have learned through countless experiences in the pastorate and recently through the cancer of my son, God might allow the body to die, but the soul will be at home with the Lord (II Corinthians 5:8).

"*But the men marvelled, saying, what manner of man is this, that even the winds and the sea obey Him?*" (Matthew 8:27) Be assured of this, sometime you too will marvel at the miracles God performs along your crossing from earth to heaven. God has not promised an awe-free sailing to the celestial shore. He has promised: "The Lord shall preserve thy going out and thy coming in from this time forth, and even for evermore." (Psalm 121:9) Stilling storms is one of God's specialties. He loves nothing better than to rebuke a demonic storm, a diseased tempest, a devilish gale. So the next time you find yourself in a sinking bark, remember these classic sermonettes from the Savior Himself.

86.

CHANGELESS CLIFF

I have only known in my life one family who ever lived on a sea cliff, the Greenlaw family of Eastport, Maine. (At the compiling of this sermonette the Greenlaw family has sold their sea-cliff bungalow and moved to Ellsworth.) Eastport was my home for five years, and in that time I had countless opportunities to visit with the Greenlaws and enjoy their own private cliff. What made it even more special is that it was a sea-cliff overlooking a rugged piece of the down east coast of Maine, some of the most spectacular seascapes I have seen in all my travels to the seashores of the world.

Recently, I returned to that cliff and had a chance, if only for a few moments, to stand and gaze again across the bay between the American Moose Island and the Canadian Campobello Island. It was a raw, windy day in March on Passamaquoddy Bay, but nothing could dampen my spirits in being back again to one of my most favorite spots on this planet, a bluff overlooking Greenlaw Beach. Returning from that short visit (I was there for the funeral of a dear parishioner of the Washington Street Baptist Church.), I came across an article from a much read author, Phillip Keller (perhaps most famous for his award-winning book "A Shepherd's Look at the 23rd Psalm"), under the title of "In the Company of Cliffs" in which he wrote: *"The rising and falling tides, the eternal impact of water on shore, the gnawing and grinding of boulders against basement formations, the rasping erosion of sand and rock laden wave chisel away at the cliffs night and day.*

Slowly, slowly, but never so surely, they are undercut. Then in some fierce blow, with rain beating against the sodden banks, the whole structure will start to shift. The end is a thundering, slithering mass of earth that slips into the sea." What Keller wrote of the cliffs of his experience isn't true everywhere.

Don't get me wrong. What Keller wrote is probably true of most sea cliffs around the world, but the cliffs of downeast Maine are made of sturdier stuff. The sea cliffs of Maine are not easily changed, but why? The reason is a simple one. Most of the sea cliffs up and down the shore of Maine are made of granite, a hard stone that resists anything the Gulf of Maine can throw against it. In one spot where I loved to walk the Greenlaw cliffs this attrition of the cliff is clearly seen. It is a high cliff (over eighty feet) that juts out into the bay, and its base is solid granite and its wall face is grey granite. Its top is covered in low bush blueberries, and it stands unaffected these hundreds of years, if not thousands. Oh, the occasional jagged piece has been knocked loose by a fierce storm or a mighty gale, but the cliff itself is far from any danger of collapsing. It has a firm foundation despite its height, and it will last as long as the sea. The salty waters of any ocean can wear and tear into any shoreline, but the granite seaside of Maine can weather any encroachment.

Like me, that cliff has strength against anything nature can throw against it because it is firmly anchored in the rock. Like the wise man in Jesus' classic parable, I too have built my faith on the Rock Christ Jesus (I Corinthians 10:4). There is something very reassuring about Jesus' analogy when he said, "I will liken him to a wise man, which built his house upon a rock; and the rain descended, and the floods came, and the wind blew, and beat upon that house; and it fell not: for it was founded upon a rock." (Matthew 7:24-25) Calvin's old cottage on Moose Island rests secure on a changeless cliff. I too rest secure on the Rock of Ages. There is no fear for those who dwell on such rocky bluffs, no matter the storm, despite the winds and waves that buffet them. Job said it best: *"To dwell in the cliffs . . . and in the rocks."* (Job 30:6)

87.

FLYING FOWL

One of the most memorable events of our trip to Nokomis, Florida, nearly twenty years ago was its marvelous beach and the fowl I saw there. I had left a nearly bird-free Maine the day before for the abundance of Florida fowl for a week. Watching the sea birds was a pleasant part of our vacation to the Sunshine State. David put it best in these verses from his eighth Psalm: "The fowl of the air, and the fish of the sea, and whatsoever passeth through the paths of the seas. O Lord our Lord, how excellent is thy name in all the earth." (Psalm 8:8-9) And that includes Florida and its flying fowl.

On the first afternoon of our mid-January trip, I witnessed the collective sounds of thousands of birds. We had stopped in a small mall to pick up a few items when I noticed the loud chirping of the fowls of Florida. It was the first sign, besides the temperature, that I knew I wasn't in Maine anymore. January in Maine might get you a peep or two from a few chickadees if you have a bird feeder out or a few caws from a lone raven who has decided to stay in the city for the winter hoping for a meal from a road-killed squirrel, but January in Florida is fowl country as most northern birds have made their way south for the year's coldest season. That evening of our first day we went out to supper and the trees near the restaurant seemed to be filled with birds settling in for a long winter vacation. I must admit, seeing it was my first time in Florida, their numbers were overwhelming because I will never forget the racket they were making that night. But for me the highlight of our trip south in the category of fowl was the shore birds I watched day after day on Nokomis and Casperson Beaches.

There seemed to be birds in the sea and birds in the air everywhere. There seemed to be birds on the beach and birds in the bushes everywhere. It seemed that in any direction you turned there were sand pipers, sea gulls, pelicans, cormorants, storks, and scores of birds I didn't even recognize. I couldn't help but stare at the myriad of fowl I saw never seeing such numbers in my life. Overwhelmed by the numbers and varieties, I simply stood in awe of the flying fowl of Florida. From the darting sand piper on the beach to the ugly pelican on the rocky breakers, I switched from one to the other watching their every movement. From the graceful gull in flight to the diving cormorant just off shore, I observed their place along the ocean's edge. No two birds acted the same way—their steps in the sand, their search for shrimp, their flight or fights, their wings beating in the air, their call to their feathered friends—each was different. Each seemed to bring to the overall pattern of the seashore a unique action and an unusual reaction.

Some birds seemed content just to soar on the warm air currents just off shore. Others were more content just to stand on an old rock formation hoping a fisherman might give them supper. Others were walking the beach in search of a snack from the incoming tide. Yet others were picking at the leftovers of those humans who had lunch on the beach. Still others were swimming and diving in the gulf waters in hopes of a seafood dinner. The more I watched the fowls of Florida, the birds on the beach, the more they looked like the people who had also flown south for the winter, people like me. There were some just content to lie around enjoying the warm sand while others were fishing in hopes of catching a fish for supper. Still others were darting in and out, to and fro in the incoming tide in search of a prize shell or a highly valued shark's tooth. And then there were those like me, swimming and diving in the refreshing waters of the Gulf of Mexico, bobbing and basking in the warmth and wonder of being a "snowbird" for a few days.

88.

FABULOUS FLOWERS

Central California where my daughter's family lives is world renowned for its mild climate and agricultural bounty. Its shores on the Pacific contain beautiful beaches, especially around Monterey Bay. It has become a mecca for millions from all over the world who love warm ocean breezes and rough Pacific surf. Up and down the seashore humanity crowds the shoreline with housing development, from the simplest house to the multi-million dollar mansion. Concrete and iron, glass and brick fill the coastline, as close as they can, but between the sand and the land are strips of ground in which trees and bushes and flowering shrubs of every kind are located. And then there are the wildflowers. Solomon wrote: "The flowers appear on the earth; the time of the singing birds is come, and the voice of the turtle is heard in our land." (Song of Solomon 2:12)

I have written often in this series of sermonettes of the birds of the beach, but rarely have I mentioned the flowering bushes, and I have yet to meet my first turtle. I know from creation that the flowers came on the third day (Genesis 1:11), but it wasn't until the fifth day for birds (Genesis 1:20) and the sixth day for the turtle (Genesis 1:24). God decided in His divine design to throw a splash of color into His new world with the introduction of the flower in all its forms and shades. In my travels in California visiting my daughter and husband and of course our grandson Judah (and now our granddaughter Elena Hope) I have seen the meadows of native grasses and the wildflowers that dot the area. Granted, your timing has to be in the wet seasons, but what a sight and what sites when they are all out together. In my last trip to Salinas I went with my daughter and grandson to a favorite beach, a park just north of the City of Monterey. It was August and the best had passed, but there was still color in the flowering shrubs and flowering bushes in the park next to Fort Ord Beach. Around the California sycamore trees were native plants and shrubs and everywhere signs not to touch or walk on or near the fragile undergrowth. In California, as in many other places around the world, these plants helped prevent erosion.

One would think in such a mild climate these fabulous flowers would have an easy time of it, but rooted in the weak soil of a coastal plain it is a tough existence. Apart from the moisture from a fog or an ocean mist, these beautiful bushes rarely see rain. The constant sun bakes the ground until it is almost concrete. Then there is the wind, that almost constant breeze off the salty sea, again conditions not ideal for growing fabulous flowers, yet despite these harsh conditions they flower. Just a simple rain on a hillside overlooking the sea will spring forth in a canopy of color as California wildflowers dot the hilltops. Even in the midst of a warming August afternoon, Marnie and Judah and I walked a concrete path to the beach with signs of spring flowers still lining the pathway. It was in April of the same year I saw the real beauty of California flowers. We had travelled west after the death of our son Scott to grieve and recover from six months of death and dying. The winter rains had turned the normally brown environment into a myriad of colors. A mantle of green covered the hills lining the Salinas Valley. Everywhere the flowers of spring were appearing, but none better than those near the Pacific Ocean. There is something in the contrast to the blue of the sea and the colors of the land. The wildflowers in the meadows and fields came in many hues and shades. There were yellows, pinks, reds, and purples in profile against the white beaches and green trees. Are you not glad that the Creator God created with shore flower? Jesus told us to "... consider the lilies of the field ..." (Matthew 6:28), even the California ones.

89.

SMOOTH STONES

Whether I walk along the seashore in America or India, one item on the beach is the same—smooth stones. Whether you walk a mile or just a few feet, normally you will find a smooth stone or two. The action of water over stone will smooth the rough and rugged edges off any piece of ledge or rock. One of the most amazing beaches I have ever visited is a small beach on the backside of Frenchboro Island off the downeast coast of Maine. What makes this beach so unique are the piles of smooth stones littering the shoreline!

All my visits to Frenchboro have been because of the Lunt family and a death in that family. I have buried them in the small hillside cemetery overlooking the inlet, and I have scattered their ashes in the bays surrounding the small island. On one of my visits as the family pastor, I was asked if I wanted to visit an unusual beach before we left. Our short trip through a stunned-spruce forest stopped at the end of a narrow path. The rest of the way we walked through a coastal terrain not unlike a few other jaunts I have taken on other islands of the rocky coast of Maine. We eventually came to a steep trail that led to a secluded beach, a beach totally exposed to the open Atlantic Ocean on the eastern end of Frenchboro. Exiting the treeline, I stood in amazement of what was before me. There unexpectedly I saw a 100-yard beach at best filled with thousands of rocks, but each rock, big or small, was a perfectly smooth stone.

The beautifully arched beach was outlined landward by a short granite cliff covered in the same stunned spruce we had walked through to get to Stony Beach. On each end of the tiny bay the granite formations of the island jutted out into the ocean. Even on this calm day in the Gulf of Maine, a strong wave action was crashing onto the beach, and I soon learned the reason for the uniqueness of the stones on the shore. The landscape created a half bowl effect resulting in the wave action churning and grinding the rocks on and near shore against themselves. The constant pounding of the surf and the resulting wave action literally smoothed every stone into a perfectly rounded rock. The weathering force of the turbulent Atlantic over time had created piles of these stones all along the beach. One could see how bits and pieces of granite broken off from the shoreline had rolled and tumbled in the washing machine of the bay until the rocks were as smooth as satin. Big boulders and small stones alike were fashioned into works of art. Every tidal surge, gale driven wave would lift the stones, shift the stone, and pound the stones against themselves and eventually rearranged their position in a pile here and a pile there. My companions on this trip told me that each and every time they had returned the beach was totally different in the arranging of the smooth stones.

Sitting on my bookshelf next to my office desk are five stones from Stony Beach. I have them on that shelf to remind me of one of my favorite stories of the Bible, David and Goliath. When I went to Israel in 2010, I had a chance to go to the brook in the Elah Valley where David probably picked up the ". . . five smooth stones . . ." (I Samuel 17:40) he took into battle against the Philistine giant. On that day as I walked the dry streambed I looked and eventually picked up five small rocks, but they were neither large enough nor smooth enough to be used by David. In a museum in Jerusalem I was shown some examples of smooth stones more like what David might have used to strike down the warrior from Gath. It wasn't until I walked along Stony Beach in Maine that I actually was able to find five smooth stones both of the size and smoothness to bring down a giant, an object lesson to the preparation of God to provide a weapon for David.

90.

STONY SHORE

Before I leave Stony Beach on the island of Frenchboro off the downeast coast of my home state of Maine I have one more sermonette for you.

I shared last time how this exposed cove lies open to the Atlantic Ocean, how the relentless surf and sledgehammer waves have battered the rocks into perfectly smooth stones, and how a thousand storms and fierce winds have created a haven for the natural manufacturing of round, smooth rocks. Bit by bit, day after day, week after week, month after month, and year after year, the rocks of Stony Beach were slowly polished and shined into stones fit for a sling. Stones under such transformation feel no pain or discomfort, but humanity does. I have just finished a two-year teaching course on the Book of Job. After years of preparation and now years of instruction, the story of Job has a new meaning to me, especially after in the midst of these lessons the good Lord sent me to Stony Beach as I dealt with the sudden and unexpected loss of my son Scott through liver and lung cancer. It was while being pounded by this trial I came to understand something Job said shortly after he lost his health and the death of not only his oldest son (Job 1:19), but all of his children: ". . . What? Shall we receive good at the hand of God, and shall we not receive evil?" (Job 2:10) A Stony Beach pounding!

Our lives are at times like the rocks on Stony Beach. Sometimes it takes calamity and loss to shape us and mold us into the man or woman God wants us to be. Sometimes it take the surge of sorrow, the pounding of problems, the stress of sickness, the grinding of grief to smooth our character and polish our integrity, to toughen our resolve and harden our will so that we might be "... conformed to the image of His Son ..." (Romans 8:29). Most of us resist and run from the storms of life because we don't want to suffer the pain. We prefer to guard our character from the onslaught of the waves of correction and the winds of adversity. We want no stress or strain to attack our rough places, unique qualities, and sharp personalities. We would rather stay rugged and rough around the corners. So we resist anything that might change us, reshape us, and mold us more to the smooth character of Christ. For the rocks on Stony Beach it is the sea that surrounds them, that changes them, but for the Christian it is the Spirit that surrounds, encircles, and begins a dramatic work in us, but we must yield to the things that the Spirit uses to smooth us into the individual saint God wants, just like He did with Job.

Most of us will avoid the cauldron of correction at any cost. We even pray that we might be delivered from the rolling, tumbling, upsetting surf of sadness, but this is the only way the Spirit has to knock those stubborn corners off our character. We sometimes plea for God to take the cup of suffering from us, but He knows that only as we are rubbed in trials and polished in tests will we be well rounded into the Christ-like character of His Son. We are living in the days of the quick fix, the instant result, the short cut, but like the stones on Stony Beach it takes time, many storms, and a patience to stay in a trying time for the duration. We need perseverance in the plight. James writes: "Behold, we count them happy which endure. Ye have heard of the patience of Job ..." (James 5:11). Most want it to be as sudden as a jagged stone today and a gemstone tomorrow. The polished stone on Stony Beach shore took years to produce and the same is true of the Christian character. It takes the tide of time, a lifetime with many trials, and tests along the way to rub off the fatal flaws of sin. Washed in the Word, swept by the Spirit, stimulated by Christ, and polished by His love and mercy, we will be like Him—smooth.

91.

BUILDING BREAKWATERS

More often than not when mankind sets his hand into the sea, it is to build some kind of breakwater or barrier against the force of the sea. Over the last few years the engineers of the world have been confronted with massive storms that have destroyed old breakwaters so they are building them stronger and higher. But as Harvey, Irma, and Marie have demonstrated, no manmade structure has proven strong enough for the power and force of a category five hurricane or even storms smaller in strength. It is amazing to me that man would even go up against "the perfect storm." I like the devotional Phillip Keller once wrote entitled "Sea Walls and Sand Piles." I also love what he wrote: "The battering of a thousand storms, the pounding of ten thousand tides, and the eternal erosion of the ocean currents can combine to reduce sea walls to rubble. Now the cement, reinforced steel, bricks, wire, tangled pipes, and broken mortar stand in wild disarray as silent reminders of how absurd it is to try to keep the sea at bay (or in the bay). Even the most ingenious sea walls eventually crash down to collapse in broken wreckage. All is for nought! All is but passing! All is change! . . . Pausing to watch the action of the waves, washing either over the wreckage of sea walls or the crumbling ruins of a small sand castle, a profound sense of pathos sweeps over me. I cannot seem to ignore them. It is impossible for me to pass them lightly. They speak to me in terms so clear and emphatic, my attention is always arrested. For here, before my gaze, in sharp, stabling severity, stand parables or spiritual truth. You simply cannot stop the sea. It is relentless. It is irresistible! Just so, you cannot continue to ignore God and His claims on your life. Lord, help me to listen and hear Your voice."

It was the Psalmist who wrote. "I will set his hand also in the sea, and his right hand in the rivers." (Psalm 89:25) God places our hands in the waters of the world to teach us of His might, His strength, and the folly of foolishly testing either. As it is with the sea so it is with the soul of man. I am no engineer or expert on sea walls, breakwaters, or any other obstacles man has designed to keep out the sea from the dikes of Holland to the levees of New Orleans, but I have observed with Keller those that are broken, those have been breached, and those that buried in sand. Whenever man puts his hand into things of the soul, he is doing it to construct some kind of wall or barrier against the influence of his Maker. On the outside many lives seem normal and controlled, yet under close examination we discover a breakwater built to keep God out. He has made it of self, selfishness, and self-centeredness. He has buried it in pride. Around this core the man has laid sins and transgressions and iniquities until the wall is deep and high and wide. All that man can construct in the way of his Saviour is put in the way. On top he adds wicked behavior, evil thoughts, and a corrupt character. When he is through, he believes that the ocean of God's love and grace will be unable to penetrate this formidable barrier.

Then it begins. The tide of God's love begins to creep up the wall. Then the undercurrent of God's grace begins to eat away at the barrier. Day after day the Spirit of God attacks the weakest parts of the breakwater, the score of excuses the structure is buried upon. Ultimately, the time comes when the flood of prayers by God's people begins to crumble the structure, and the mercy of God breeches the defenses, and faith takes hold. In the end forgiveness sweeps the barrier away as easily as the tide clears a pile of sand off the local beach. When will we realize that God's love is just like the sea sweeping a sand castle away in the rising tide when it comes to the resistance of man.

92.

SOUTHERN STORM

I had come up with these two titles for this sermonette from the seashore: "The Tale of Five Foggy Coconut Shrimp" or "The Red, Red Robin goes Bob, Bob Bobbing Along," but in the end I decided on the title printed above and this verse from the Book of Isaiah: "For thou hast been a strength to the poor, a strength to the needy in his distress, A REFUGE FROM THE STORM [emphasis added], a shadow from the heat, when the blast of the terrible ones is as a storm against the wall." (Isaiah 25:4)

On the eve of a southern storm in Florida, my wife and I along with our travelling companions, Danny and Lori Clark, went for a boat ride up the inland waterway along the western gulf coast of the Sunshine State. Our destination for this vacation excursion was a locally famous restaurant in the area that was known for its excellent seafood. Some other friends made the journey by car, but we decided to take the scenic, seaway route and go by motorboat that some might call a yacht. The trip up was wonderful and picturesque. The inland waterway was lined with beautiful mansions, and the seascape was divine. Once we arrived it wasn't long before our orders came. Danny had ordered the coconut shrimp, and Gill (the owner of the boat) had ordered a pasta dish with shrimp. When the meal finally arrived there were only five, small shrimp on Danny's huge plate. Gill commented he was afraid that it was his lunch. Needless to say, the five shrimp were the start of many a joke including the wish that Jesus was there to multiply the five, small shrimp. I had heard of such places where the miniature size of a meal was the norm, but I never thought I would ever dine in such a place. We finished the tasty, if not bountiful meal, and headed back home. However, as we started back over the forty miles of waterway to our boat slip, the fog began to settle in. It was a slow, damp trip home, but we eventually arrived although to this day the journey will be remembered for five, thin shrimp covered in coconut.

Once we got back to our home away from home, cottage #270, everybody at the Royal Coachman Park seemed worried about the coming storm. The big fear was that there might be a tornado embedded in the heart of the storm. For my wife and I the fog had lifted and the late afternoon turned into the best day of the trip. Some other friends in the senior citizen's retirement development had lent Coleen and me bikes so we decided to take a spin around the massive trailer park. I had followed my wife's Schwinn around a couple of corners before I spotted them. A group of robins had landed under a stand of southern pine. As they worked themselves around the grassy area, all that I could think off was that classic old tune about "the red, red robin goes bob, bob bobbing along." I knew it would be at least three more months in Maine before I would see another robin so I enjoyed them a bit longer than normal. I also noticed that they didn't seem to be concerned about the up and coming storm so why should I? The flock eventually flew off to a better feeding ground, and I took up the pursuit of a Sarasota Schwinn.

Later that evening the wind began to blow heavily from the west through the pine grove we were nestled in. A few pine cones began to drop on the roof of our half-trailer as if someone was knocking. Coleen looked at me and I looked at her, but we said nothing. The rain began to pound on the roof, but for us it didn't seem excessive. Eventually, we headed for bed tired from our Florida adventures for that day. We slept through the storm to wake to another warm and sunny day. The grounds were wet and the roadways were covered in pine nettles, but no damage could be seen. God is so good!

93.

TEMPESTUOUS TIDE

"*Nevertheless the men rowed hard to bring it to the land; but they could not for the sea wrought, and was tempestuous against them.*" (Jonah 1:13) Until I witnessed the power of a Passamaquoddy Bay tide and storm, I never fully understood what the mariners of Jonah's boat were up against.

A tempestuous tidal storm has a strong tug unlike any other force I had experienced on dry land. There is a unique and unusual power that pulls from below as well as the force that draws from above. I had faced winds, both a summer gale and a winter blizzard, but neither could literally pick you up and carry you away. But a tempestuous tide and a terrible wind can do that very thing in the bay off Eastport, Maine. I will never forget the first time I felt that irresistible tug, that invincible draw.

I had not lived in the coastal community on Moose Island very long before I was asked to go fishing in the bay. I was taken to Head Harbor off the eastern tip of Campobello Island, Canada. I was first surprised when our captain (Peter Ricker) said that we couldn't even anchor in the area because the water was so deep (over 300 feet). What struck me next was the calmness of the sea. There were no winds that day so why would we have any troubles. No storms in sight! It was a lovely day in August and the sea was as still as a mill pond on a summer's eve. Even the tide was slack when we got to Peter's favorite fishing hole. It was low tide, and we were going to fish in the very narrow window of a tidal change. The ebb tide was over, and the flood tide was ready to move into the bay from the Atlantic Ocean.

As we drifted off Head Harbor Lighthouse, each drift seemed to me to happen that much quicker than the last. At first, I didn't notice it, but very soon it became clear that we were covering our fishing ground more rapidly than before. It wasn't long before we barely had enough time to get our "Christmas tree" (a series of five hooks on the end of a very long line with colorful plastic coverings to attract the Pollock near the bottom of the bay) over the side of the boat and to the bottom before we had to retrieve them. Within the hour we couldn't hold our position over the best grounds at all, and eventually our captain had to yield to the all-powerful tide. He had learned after many years fishing in that narrow inlet that it was the one force of nature that couldn't be conquered, just like trying to stop a nor'easter from coming up the coast of Maine.

Jonah and his friends on that galley to Tarshish learned in the tempestuous sea they were in that rowing against the tide was enviably impossible. How often have we tried to resist the under riding current of God's will? Was that not in reality what Jonah was doing on that ship? Granted, he was in the midst of a Mediterranean tempest, but he was also running from God's commission to Nineveh. I myself have rowed against God's will only to exhaust myself in the attempt. For three years I resisted God's will to become a pastor, but in the end, like with the mariners of Jonah's Mediterranean yacht, I yielded to the enviable. Drifting into the deep waters of His grace, I had no anchor long enough or strong enough to hold my position. And why should I? Like with the flood tide of Passamaquoddy Bay, it carried us home. If we had wanted to, we could have floated into Eastport Harbor on the back of the incoming tide. When will we realize the will of God is carrying us to "the haven of rest?" That "all things work for good," and a tempestuous tide is just drawing us back into God's perfect will. Jonah was going in the wrong direction. A tempestuous tide is sometimes just a simple "mid-course correction . . . !"

94.

HAWAII HOP

I have been to Hawaii twice in my life. Hawaii is perhaps the closest place to the Garden of Eden that I have visited in my life.

It was the summer of 1972, and my cousin Bob and I were off to a short-term missionary adventure to the land downunder. We were to spend two and a half months working with an Aboriginal tribe in the Gibson Desert of Western Australia. To get to our mission field we literally had to fly half way around the world. From the northern hemisphere to the southern hemisphere we went from summer to winter and back again. Starting from our hometown of Perham in northern Maine, we eventually arrived at the remote mission station of Warburton Range, a United Aboriginal Mission complex in the middle of the Gibson Desert, three hundred miles north, west, south, and east from any habitable town. If you get out your old world globe and put your left finger on Presque Isle (where we flew from), Maine, and then put your right finger on Warburton, Australia, you will discover that your two fingers are directly opposite each other. But to get to our final destination, we had to go through Hawaii.

It was also my first experience with the vastness of the Pacific Ocean. Being from landlocked Maine (northern Maine) at the time, I hadn't seen much of any ocean. From the west coast of the United States (Los Angeles, California) we flew directly to Honolulu. We were there only long enough to change planes for an overnight flight to Sydney, Australia. Because we had followed the sun all day, it was still light when we flew in from the sea to the Hawaiian Islands. They were beautiful against the backdrop of the Pacific Ocean. I could see from my first glimpse why so many people enjoy spending their vacation time there. I even had a college friend who many years later contacted me about his first missionary calling. I expected him to say New Guinea or Africa, but to my surprise he said Hawaii! I laughed because of my two experiences passing through, but I will never forget his reply, *"Even paradise needs missionaries!"* He was right, and he would later minister on a number of islands in the South Pacific.

With barely an hour layover both coming and going, about all I was able to enjoy of Hawaii were the flights in and out and a few views from the airport. Ten weeks later when we flew back through Hawaii on our way home back to Maine, the approach was different coming in from the South Pacific. The islands were like a chain of emeralds against the bluish, greenish sea. My heart was struck again with the loveliness and the lushness of the vegetation on these rocks in the middle of the huge body of water. But as with our outbound flight, our stay was short and sweet. I don't know why we did not stay for a few days. I guess we just were anxious to get home to our girlfriends (ladies we would marry within the year) and family. To my memory I don't even remember discussing the opportunity to stay a bit longer and see a few things up close and personal so the last thing I saw of paradise was a backward glimpse through a jet plane's window as we reached a cruising altitude above the clouds.

I have never returned though I hope I might at least visit Pearl Harbor (on my bucket list). My brief encounter with paradise has often reminded me of our first parents Adam and Eve. I wonder how often they pondered their brief stay in the best place God ever created for mankind. They were in such a hurry to fulfill their desires for what they were convinced was better, to be like God (Genesis 3:5), that they rushed through the best place they would ever experience. I am convinced, so did I.

95.

SCOTT'S SEAGLASS

Seaglass has played a rather unusual role in our family this pass year. I write this sermonette from the seashore on the first anniversary of my wife's and my trip to bring our son Scott home from North Carolina. It seems hard to believe that a year has already passed since we got the news that our son was dying of cancer (he would last just six short months). Our first time away from him after his passing was to the Jersey Shore to deal with our grief and loss. It was on Long Beach that I found a piece of sea glass. The minute I saw it I knew what I would eventually do with it. Just a few months ago I took that broken piece of wave-washed glass and placed it into the hands of a jeweler to create a necklace for my wife. In a creative and imaginative way he shaped a discarded, broken object that now brings a constant reminder to Scott's mother of the bond of love they shared. As the Apostle Paul writes, "For now we see through a glass darkly; but then face to face: now I know in part; but then shall I know as also I am known." (I Corinthians 13:12) Scott's sea glass speaks of the low tides of life and the roaring surf of suffering, but also of quiet interludes in the company of one we cherished dearly.

As I ponder the sea glass necklace that now adorns my wife's neck, I see in the refection of that glass the life of my son Scott, once a whole bottle, complete and full of life, but the day came a little over a year ago when his body was broken into a million pieces with the devastating news that at the age of 39 he had an aggressive lung and liver cancer that would without doubt take his life within a year. Shattered and broken into pieces, he tried with all his strength and will power to hold his life together. Normality changed almost immediately because this carefree spirit, who loved the out-of-doors, golf courses, fishing holes, and open roads driving his Harley, was over. The new normal was a hospital room, test after test, treatment after treatment that only got him sicker with more pain and discomfort. His life was like that bottle broken and dumped into the turbulence of the surf. Each edge was pointy and sharp, but tide by tide, breaker by breaker, rolling surf by rolling surf, wave by wave, his body was pounded and the corners were smoothed and the glass was polished for a new world. After weeks of fighting and months of struggle, the final product was ready to be found face to face with God. Scott's final trip was a heavenly journey to a land of painless days and a cancer-free life with his Maker. What was left behind was a symbol of that final battlefield war, a shard of glass, a piece of sea glass found on the sea shore at Long Beach Island, New Jersey.

All this might sound a bit ordinary, imaginary, but the minute I gave Coleen this piece of sea glass, she understood everything I was trying to say with the gift. Some call them a keepsake, a memento, an air loom, but for Coleen and me it is much more. Perhaps, only those who have had to bury a child can relate to the symbolism this sea glass necklace represents. In a small way it represents our son's life because he spent most of it in a very heavy surf. His was not an easy life after he left home for the world. Granted, the troubled seas he spent the bulk of his last twenty years in were of his own doing. Yet through it all he took every blow, every turn of the tide with grace and pleasantness. As we have said time and time again, through every painful period he never complained. You would think a piece of broken glass would be sharp and hard to handle, but Scott was a complete joy to take care of during his final 183 days, the amount of days his mother and I personally cared for him. In the end I didn't see a broken, bruised body. I saw a beautiful, polished piece of sea glass ready to be worn around the neck of the Almighty.

96.

SEASHORE SUNRISE

Did you know that ten times in the Bible the phrase "... *toward the sunrising*..." (Numbers 21:11, 34:15; Deuteronomy 4:41, 47; Joshua 1:15, 13:5, 19:12, 19:27, 19:34; Judges 20:43) is found? For any sea lover the most wonderful interlude of the day is when the sun comes up out of the ocean. I know for most it is at the setting of the sun when the sun sinks into the sea, but for me the morning is best. Just two days ago I got a text from my daughter and her family with a few pictures. The Legaspi's were enjoying an afternoon on Salinas River Beach in sunny, central California. I was more interested in the kite flying abilities of my two year old grandson, but I was impressed with the beautiful sunset picture sent at the end of a series of photographs. Granted, sunrise or sunset the experience is breathtaking, but again as for me I prefer looking "toward the sunrising" and here are the reasons why.

A sunrising over a sea is usually a private affair. Be honest with me. How many sunsets over a sea have you enjoyed with a crowd? I remember well the sunset I had with my daughter on our last day in India on Eve's Beach in Kerala State in 2007. Granted, the seashore wasn't as crowded as the middle of the afternoon, but there were still plenty of beachcombers enjoying the blazing ball dying on the horizon. Yet on my very first sunrising on Long Beach on the Jersey shore just this past spring in 2017, I was alone except for a dedicated surf fisherman and two lonely beach walkers. Most times in these early hours of the dawn the coastline is void of human life. There are no beach balls being tossed about, no children yelling and screaming in an out of the surf, no loud music, just a stillness and solitude. The feverish frenzy of the crowd is missing and peace pervades the sea, the shore, the surf. Gently the eastern sky turns from a darkish grey to a golden yellow and eventually to a burning red. At first the reflected light casts deep shadows over the coastline, the rocks, sand dunes, and trees, if there are any, are silhouetted against the shore. Everything along the beach stands in sharp contrast to the heavenly light creeping slowly over the distant horizon. The long slender rays of light reach into every structure along the shore, touching every tree, cliff, bluff, and resting bird waiting for the light to take flight. With each passing moment the seascape is being bathed in a golden glow, but if there are clouds on the horizon the light will change a hundred times into prisms of crimson and yellow and more.

As one gazes towards the sunrising, a sweet hush engulfs the beach. The sand that has been swept by the night tide will take on an unmatched glow. They say that God never duplicates a sunrise? Each is different and distinct from any other. I don't know if that is true because I have only witnessed a few sunrises over a sea in my life, but I know the ones that I have seen were different. Each bore a unique beauty and similitude of its own whether along the coast of Maine or the coastline of New Jersey. For me the sunrising of a new day are like the new day. Each will be inscribed differently. No day in my life has been exactly the same as a yesterday in my past. What will be the highlights of this day? What will I underline at the end of this day that stood out to me? Each sunrising in my life whether on a sea shore or an inland field breaks anew in my soul with the promise that "This is the day which the Lord hath made . . ." (Psalm 118:24) This is a special gift from the Almighty, just like the sunrise, for me to cherish, claim, and conquer. It is a wonderful treasure of time that I can use to serve Him, glorify Him, and honor Him. It has not been given to squander so as I look toward the sunrising I remember Him.

97.

COASTLINE CONVERSATIONS

I know that the word conversation in Philippians 3:20 ("*For our conversation is in heaven; for whence also we look for the Saviour, the Lord Jesus Christ.*") is talking about our citizenship in the heavenlies, but I would like to make this application to the wonderful privilege we have to communicate with our Lord and Saviour any time, any place. Maltbie Babcock, in her marvelous church hymn, "This is My Father's World," speaks of this ability and reality with these words: ". . . in the rustling grass I hear Him pass, He speaks to me everywhere!" Can I share a few coastline conversation concepts I have learned from the Almighty over the years along the seashores I have strolled?

In our media crazy world we have lost the ability to see God everywhere and to hear God anywhere. I love anything Indian (the country of India) because of my five trips to the subcontinent. I was reading once of a missionary who worked in the poverty that is India, the squalor that can be found in all Indian cities and the degradation that is the normal life of the average citizen of India's hinterland. Very early in this missionary's time in India, he taught his children these valuable lessons: *"Learn to look. Observe quietly. Think long thoughts. Find what is beautiful. Give humble thanks. Recall it to mind often. Refresh your soul in the gentle stream of our Father's bounty!"* I think I would only add one thought to his marvellous list: *Talk to God regularly.* We must learn to live in the attitude of the continual and constant presence of God whether in a sanctuary or on a seashore, whether in a chapel or on a coastline, God is there. He is talking, but are we listening? We must have our eyes open and our ears listening to see and hear the fragments of conversation embedded in the coastlines we walk, to search, seek, and then seize every word the Lord "declares" (Psalm 19:1). I like the observation that Phillip Keller made in his book "Sea Edge." "We of the West have, by our crude and crass culture become so conditioned to look for the sensational and spectacular in our experiences that we miss seeing the stars while looking for our spacecraft!" Could I make this application to this concept? We also miss hearing "the still small voice of God" on the beach while listening to "rock and roll" by the Beach Boys.

When did we forget that God's talks to us are not confined to the Bible? Babcock again writes, "This is my Father's world, the birds their carols raise, the morning light, the lily white, declare their Maker's praise." When did we forget that our conversations with God are not only in our churches? Babcock again, "This is my Father's world, and to my listening ear all nature sings, and round me rings the music of the spheres." When did we forget that the Almighty is not restricted to our creeds or our liturgy? Babcock: "This is my Father's world; O let me never forget that though the wrong seems oft so strong, God is the Ruler yet!" We have forgotten that God is on every beach we walk, and we can meet Him in a thousand ways, at every turn of the trail. Babcock: "This is my Father's world: I rest me in the thought of rocks and trees, of skies and seas His hand the wonders wrought!" Only those who believe this will hear God's voice in the surf, recognize God talking in a sea breeze, or pick up a heavenly conversation as one walks a coastline. It can be for us a wholesome, spirit-filled, and maybe a holy experience when we take time to spend a little time, an interlude, talking and walking with God on our morning stroll along a sandy strand on any seashore. If we will but pause once in a while in mid-stride and recognize the voice of God ". . . speaks to me everywhere."

98.

IDEALIC ISLAND

I will finish this series of sermonettes from the seashore by returning in my mind to the only real time I actually lived surrounded by seascape, rocky beaches, and rugged shoreline. Those were the years (1986-1991) I lived and ministered on an island off the downeast coast of Maine. I had gone there to recover from thirteen years of difficult pastoring, and I found Isaiah's admonition to be true: "Keep silence before me, O islands; and let the people renew their strength . . ." (Isaiah 41:1) It was there I renewed my strength for the pastoral ministry, and I did because I am now in my forty-fifth year.

If I live to be a hundred, and I have no aspiration to do that, I shall never forget what Moose Island did for me and my family during the most difficult period in my life's work. After two life-changing pastorates, the good Lord in His wise providence led me and my loved ones to the people and place of the Washington Street Baptist Church in Eastport, Maine. I will be honest and tell you that I questioned God's move to send me to an out-of-the-way town (a former city) on an out-of-the-way island in the middle of Passamaquoddy Bay. Despite being a native Maineaic, I must admit I didn't even know that the island existed when I was first contacted by the pulpit committee of the church. Yet my heavenly Father knew exactly what I needed, and what I needed was an island, a granite coastline and a rocky shoreline. I needed gale-force winds, coastal nor'easters, and isolation. I needed the tides, the waves, the beaches, the cliffs, and the bluffs.

Moose Island has produced in me a grateful gratitude to my Father for the renewal and restoration it gave me while I was there. Again and again and again I have thought of my half-decade there, and each time there has come from my innermost being a thanksgiving beyond description. Besides renewal of strength there was a restoration of inspiration and revelation. It was on that idealistic island I found and came to love the therapy of writing. It was the year 1988, and I am just a few days away from my 29th anniversary (November 1), the day I wrote my first remembrance. When I finished I thought I would never write again, but I never stopped writing. I attribute it all to the atmosphere and aria of the coast. The combination of tempestuous tides and beach breakers stirred in me again the love of preaching and teaching the Bible. The view from an island surrounded by islands was both pleasant and peaceful. It was there my God put a new song in my heart, a new passion in my talk, and a new love for God's people. I must admit I nearly lost all three, but walking the shores of Eastport restored them all and more.

No matter where I stood on that island I could see the sea's edge. Oh, at times it might be blocked by fog, low clouds, or rain, but what I couldn't see I could hear in the sounds of the sea and its shore. The sea was never beyond my reach or the reach of my senses. It was there I learned there is an energy, a therapy, and vitality from wind and water, sea and surf. It is an environment that engulfs you, surrounds you, embraces you, and carries you on its strong shoulders. I learned that the sea edge is a special place filled with sweet people and unlimited sermons. I still hear the sea even though I live ten miles from it now. At my best, I am still an islander in heart, and I shall never forget the impression the sea, the seashore, and the seafarers had on my life. As Phillip Keller so fitly wrote of it years ago, *"So I am stilled before its majesty. My soul is silent in its presence. There is assurance in its might."* I say so long from the seashore because it seems that the good Lord is leading me farther from its shore, but I hope never too far that I can't return. I might not see or hear its melody today, but its songs and sermons still vibrate in my soul.

SERMON FROM THE SURF

As you have noticed by now, the sea has for most of my life drawn me into its mighty, yet meek magnetism. The combination of wind and wave and water has called my soul and beckoned my spirit to its seaside, its shoreline, and its sandy sod for decades now. Its sermons, not always audible at times, have moved me to write them down and now I have, but I have one final set of thoughts, remembrances, and meditations I would like to share of the magnificent majesty that comes from a seashore sermonette or in this case "a sermon from the surf:" ". . . *What ailed thee, O thou sea . . . ?*" (Psalm 114:5)

Though I have made countless visits to the oceans of the world, my awe of them has never waned and my wonder of them has never dimmed. Whether the rough and rugged Atlantic Ocean in my own backyard of coastal Maine, the tranquil and tame Indian Ocean off the shores of my adopted country of Kerala, India, or the broad and bluish Pacific Ocean near my daughter's backyard by Monterey Bay, every time I step on one of their shores their wide expanse and their distant horizon draws in my entire being. The grandeur and greatness of the space humbles me every time as I stand barefoot in their sand. I have always been a man of open spaces, long views, and natural vistas. That is why I love the North Maine Woods, a place of few people, massive tree stands, and sparkling brooks teeming with brook trout, and tranquility and solitude unmatched, except perhaps on an isolated beach void of humanity. These ingredients are as important to my being as the air I breathe, the food I eat, and the water I drink. To think I would have to stay cramped in a man-made city for all my life would be a death sentence to me. There are times I just have to get to the wood, go to the shore, get away from it all, and find an alone space where it is just God and me. Perhaps it is how I was raised, my upbringing on a potato and dairy farm in northern Maine, but just maybe, it is what I have learned from "the carpenter of Nazareth," "the stranger from Galilee." ". . . Come ye yourselves apart into a desert place, and rest a while: for there were many coming and going and they had no leisure so much as to eat . . ." (Mark 6:31) Jesus' "desert place" was by a sea.

I have learned in my study of the topography of Galilee that when Jesus found an isolated place it more often than not had direct sight to the Sea of Galilee. The day Jesus fed the five thousand (Matthew 14:15-21), He finished the day by sending His disciples off across that inland sea (Matthew 14:22). After Jesus had sent the multitude away, He climbed a nearby hill to rest and pray (Matthew 14:23), but it was from that hill Jesus would later see His disciples in trouble on the sea (Matthew 14:24-25). The end result was Jesus' famous stroll on the sea (Matthew 14:26-33), but for me it is the reality that Jesus' quiet places often overlooked the sea. When I lived on Moose Island off the downeast coast of Maine, I had a favorite walking trail to a place the locals called Shackerford's Head. From those sea cliffs you could look out upon the sea. It became a mediating and pondering place for me during my five-year stay. As I watched the tide come in and the surf increase, I heard the "still small voice" of God loud and clear. How many surf sermons I heard are still to be recorded? The muted sounds of the sea from that spot still echo in my mind. Over time it became a pilgrimage for me to climb the hill and get "a glimpse of glory bright" from the sea edge off Passamaquoddy Bay. Whether from the actual sea edge on a sandy shore like Greenlaw Beach or the sky edge from a seaside cliff off Shackerford's Head, each time was a sermon from the surf for me. *"He that hath an ear, let him hear what the Spirit saith unto the . . ."* (Revelation 2:7)

www.ingramcontent.com/pod-product-compliance
Lightning Source LLC
Chambersburg PA
CBHW062036220426
43662CB00010B/1526